THE MAN WHO DEFUSES BOMBS

HOW TO MASTER COMMERCIAL
DISPUTES AND ESCALATIONS....
AND HOW TO AVOID THEM IN
THE FIRST PLACE

ASHLEY SALTZMAN

Foreword

I am delighted to be asked to write the Foreword to Ashley's book, *The Man Who Defuses Bombs*, but then I am biased.

Ashley worked for me at SAP when I was Senior Vice-President of SAP Services (Asia-Pacific Japan) and he managed all of the major commercial escalations across the region in those four years. He saved SAP millions of dollars/euros in troubled situations, whether they were projects in delivery, overdue receivables, or when there was a lack of clarity about what was committed versus delivered as customer experience.

Ashley's approach to commercial dispute resolution and escalations is second to none. He shows that, to get the best for a customer and your business or organisation, you need to play as a team, respect standards and principles, and not just solve individual issues. This is what 'defusing the bomb' is all about.

He shows you that it's better to be proactive during the structuring of deals and engagements, rather than reactive and hoping for the best from partners – this is the 'how to avoid disputes' part of the book.

Everything Ashley covers in his book he puts into practice himself every day – I have seen it first-hand.

Ashley is truly an expert in his field, most professional and with calm composure. In his book, he shares more than 20 years of experience, knowledge and insights that you can apply from the moment you finish reading it. He is just a great leader from whom you will definitely learn so much.

Michiel Verhoeven
Managing Director, SAP UK and Ireland

Contents

Introduction	01
What will you learn from this book?	03

Part 1 – Don't let the facts get in the way of a good story   **06**
    How to gather the facts   09
    The five key questions   11
    Let's summarise   14

Part 2 - How to avoid commercial escalations   **15**
    The four-step approach to start a new investigation   **18**

    Documentation   **21**
      Tip – Sample email to send after an informal meeting   25

    Communication   **27**
      Failure to communicate is not an option   29
      Don't wait to share bad news   30
      Executives don't like surprises   32
      Tip – Sample email for communicating bad news   34
      When crafting an email, less is more   35
      Tip – What should be included in an executive briefing?   37
      Don't forget to pick up the phone   38

    Accountability   **39**
      My three key 'accountability' rules: 40
      Let's summarise   42

Part 3 – How to manage commercial escalations (when it's too late to avoid) — 44

The Relationship — 47
Trust – it takes years to gain, but just one wrong move to lose — 47
Tip – What to do first when you get involved in an escalation — 50
How do you handle unhappy clients? — 51
The first meeting — 54
The process for gathering the facts — 56
How do you ensure you get to the truth? — 57
Let's summarise — 61

The Approach — 63
Strategy + Approach = Outcome — 63
There is no 'one' approach — 65
Who's who in the zoo — 66
Preparing for the meeting — 67
Whom do you need on your team? — 71
The importance of being face-to-face — 73
Leave your ego at the door — 76
How to keep your emotions out of the room — 78
How to deal with personal attacks — 81
Tip – Steps to deal with a personal attack — 83
The order to raise issues — 84
Lose the fear of upsetting the client — 85
Beware of personal agendas — 88
Let's summarise — 89

The Negotiation — 90
Asking for too much — 90
Tip – Shifting the conversation and the negotiation — 92
Ways to influence a negotiation stalemate — 94
Let's summarise — 98

The lifecycle of commercial disputes and escalations — 99

About Ashley — 101

About The Program — 105

Introduction

Let's face it, fixing problems is not what most of us like to do. In fact, most of us like to give that task to someone else. I'm the opposite. I like to solve problems and I run into challenges all the time.

In my work and life, I am what many would call a realist-optimist. I see things for what they are, no matter how good or not so good. I don't see problems, only challenges, and I am always optimistic about my ability to solve them.

I use the term 'not so good' instead of the word 'bad' because that's me the realist, and I always see the glass as half-full rather than half-empty – that's me the optimist.

My approach to the issues that life presents is that there is no problem that can't be solved. It is finding the solution or resolution that poses the real challenge.

In business, this is even more the case when a resolution has to be acceptable to all parties involved and impacted. Dealing with multiple parties certainly makes crafting a resolution more challenging, but it doesn't change my fundamental belief that there is no problem that can't be solved.

When you think about it, the reality for everyone is that a lot of things go wrong a lot of the time. How well you manage these challenges will determine if the outcome is a success. And, if it is a business problem, then success is measured by the outcome you achieve based on the strength of your relationship with your client. A positive outcome can not only see you maintain the present relationship, but in many situations even build on it and develop an even stronger future with them. In my world, business relationships are defined by the way you manage an escalation or dispute situation.

I've spent over 20 years defusing commercial bombs, both large and small, across a range of different industries, countries and complexities. I've built up a toolkit of techniques, knowledge and insights into human behaviour that I want to share with you so that you're better equipped from the outset to tackle the commercial problems that will inevitably come your way.

As a result, you will become a more effective and valuable manager and executive – whether your role is sales, delivery, projects or commercial.

So let's get started.

What will you learn from this book?

The aim of this book is to help you to get better at dealing with situations that go wrong. For anyone in a client-facing role – sales or delivery, managers or non-managers – if you are someone who manages relationships, then you are in a position to make a difference because you can see problems in their early stages, at the very beginning, sometimes even before they start to happen. As I like to say, you can see the storm coming.

With the right knowledge and skills, you have the best opportunity to help rectify these situations – find out what the problem really is and sort it out before it becomes something bigger.

In this book I share insights, tips, techniques and advice to help you deal with the problem situations that lead to disputes and escalations.

Now, before you delve into the content, I want to spend a few minutes making sure we all understand the important terminology I use regularly throughout the book.

Time and again I will use favourite words and terms – these are definitely not dictionary definitions, which means in some cases you will find them interchangeable.

A **'Problem Situation'** is when an issue arises that needs to be resolved. If addressed quickly, the problem becomes nothing more than just that and there are no further steps to be taken.

However when it is not addressed in a timely manner, it becomes an escalation.

An **'Escalation'** is when a problem situation has not been resolved – that is, it is either unresolved, or resolved but not to the client's satisfaction. It becomes an escalation when the problem situation needs involvement at a more senior level of management, and in my world that is the first step towards a dispute.

A **'Dispute'** is between two or more parties who are in disagreement. It is when the escalation is raised to a higher level of intensity. A dispute typically arises after an escalation has still not been resolved despite the involvement of senior levels of management.

In the technology environment, these terms may relate to project delivery – the actual delivery of services to run the project.

'Commercial Escalation'. Many people think that a reference to commercial escalation means contracts, pricing and negotiation While it does have an element of each of these things, a commercial escalation is something different.

It is when an escalation impacts the commercial relationship between two companies – for example, a vendor and their client. The escalation may pose a threat to future sales opportunities, a project being delivered or the overall engagement with the client.

All of the key points that I raise in the book are things that have gone wrong or have been done wrong, and they will cause or have caused disputes and escalations. That is, each of the topics that I cover is something that people or teams have done wrong in the past, which contributed to or directly caused a problem that led to an escalation. They have been done wrong many times in multiple projects by multiple people across many companies for many years.

Each point that you will read about comes from mistakes that I discovered when investigating a case. Each of these elements led to an escalation. These are my learnings from more than 23 years of experience in cleaning up the mess that others created.

What I would like you to think about and take away from each topic is that when we stop making these mistakes or when we do things better, we reduce the chance of an escalation.

Part 1

Don't let the facts get in the way of a good story

When you speak to different people involved in a situation that has gone wrong, you always get different versions of what happened. People love jazzing up a story, often adding a bit of colour to make it even more interesting. However, when it comes to disputes and escalations, it is only the facts that matter.

Rule number one when dealing with any dispute or escalation is that you need to understand what actually happened. It is extremely important to separate fact, interpretation and perception.

This is explained as the difference between objective and subjective truths. Objective is what actually happened based on the facts, whereas subjective is what you think happened based on the facts, but it relies on assumptions, beliefs and opinions, and is influenced by emotions and personal feelings.

Have you ever wondered why the police and lawyers want to interview multiple people who have witnessed the same event? It is because everyone has a different perspective, despite the fact that what they have seen is the same event. The same applies when there is a commercial problem. Different people have a different perspective.

When investigating a situation in dispute, it is critical that you strip away the commentary, stories, opinions and added extras. Allow each person to share their version of what happened, remembering that they will each see the situation from their own perspective.

It's also critical to understand that people will be emotionally invested in their own perspective to a greater or lesser degree, depending on a range of factors including their own personality, level and sense of responsibility, accountability, confidence and sometimes fear.

My approach to solving any problems, commercial or otherwise, is to focus on the facts and the facts alone.

It is hard for anyone to argue against the facts when everyone knows that is what happened. The challenge is to ask the right people the right questions so that the facts become clear.

Even after determining the facts, people often continue to push their version of the story, knowing that it's not what actually happened but because it suits their cause and supports their argument. People can argue whatever they want the truth to be, but that won't stand up against a fact-based approach if it's not the truth.

As the first step in dealing with any dispute or escalation, it is extremely important to get a clear understanding of what actually happened and in what order.

As we have already established, the more people you interview, the more you can expect to get different versions of or variations on 'the truth'. In a commercial situation there will also be different groups of people – the client, your company, and sometimes a third-party supplier. Somewhere in the middle of all these perspectives lies the truth.

You need to determine the version that is the truth, and to do that there is a very structured process you have to follow to achieve the right outcome. It has to result in getting a clear understanding of what actually happened.

You can only do that by conducting a series of interviews with many of the people who were involved. Once you have gathered the facts, you piece together the evidence or proof that supports those facts.

How to gather the facts

Here is the technique I use to gather the facts - with some commentary thrown in:

1. Interview up to three people from each of the parties involved in the situation; for example, if there is your company, the client and a third-party supplier, then you should aim to interview at least two and ideally three people from each organisation – that means six to nine interviews. This will give you enough to pick up variations and inconsistencies in each story.

2. Conduct your interviews one-on-one with the same list of starting questions for each of them; what you are trying to find out is which facts are consistent amongst them all and which are the inconsistencies or outliers. The reason why you don't interview in groups is because you want each person to share only their own version of the story.

   The group dynamic allows people to be influenced by each other as they recount what happened. You don't want anyone to compromise their story, or make a statement based on something they heard from someone else.

3. Facts that are consistent among a number of the interviewees can be relied upon as confirmation of what actually happened – in other words, if their stories pretty much align, then you can consider this is what happened.

4. The outliers are the ones that need to be scrutinised, these are the facts where there are inconsistencies. You need to think about where these inconsistencies came from.

Why did only one person or just a few people say this?

Why didn't anyone else raise these points?

Were they there and did they see it for themselves?

Did it even happen?

Outliers raise suspicions about whether it actually happened. They require more digging.

5. As you gather the facts, you need to document all the information that has been given to you by the various parties

6. It is likely you will need to undertake two or three rounds of investigations and interviews until you get a consistent position from all parties on what actually happened.

The sole objective of this process is to put together a complete set of facts based on everyone's input. You then need to play that back to all the key parties and have them understand that these are the facts on which you are basing your position.

Not everyone will agree with everything, and you may have to agree to disagree with some people. However, if you are confident that the facts are accurate then you need to put them forward and make it clear that based on those facts you will be forming your position. You can then start to work towards resolution.

The comprehensive process that you have followed to get a clear understanding of the facts makes it very difficult for anyone to argue that something didn't happen. And any facts that don't stack up would already have been found out during your investigation.

You will also learn that people's egos often make them want to continue to argue the facts, especially when you didn't completely agree with their version of events. Remember that they are arguing their perspective - which doesn't make them wrong – but when it comes to the facts, it either happened or it didn't.

The investigation process is much more important that just identifying the facts. Arguing a position based on the agreed facts removes most of the emotion, something you will see as we work through the approach to getting a resolution. The best way to deal with any emotions along the way is to keep taking people back to the facts.

The reality is that when you have a solid understanding of the facts, then your discussions about the solution to the issue or dispute can be based on them, and not people's opinion or perspective.

The five key questions

As you have now started to understand, facts are the foundation of managing any escalation or dispute. They need to underpin all discussions, and to support your position when it is challenged or argued against. The facts enable you to argue based on what happened rather than emotions.

I have explained the technique that I use for gathering the facts. You need to do this with a purpose in mind, to help put a picture together.

The following are the five key questions that should complete that picture:

1. What has been promised to the client?
2. What has been delivered?
3. Is there a gap?
4. What is the business impact?
5. What is your/your company's exposure or commercial risk?

Let's work through these questions in some detail:

1. **What has been promised to the client?**
   You need to go back to the contract and be very clear about what requirements and expectations were set with the client before and at the time of signing it.

   Intent is extremely relevant so, in addition to the contract, you must determine what was presented and discussed during the sales process. This allows you to review all of the materials that were shared and presented.

   All of this information is critical as it represents the promises and commitments made to the client and on which their expectations are based.

2. **What has been delivered?**
   Now that you know what was promised, consider whether your company has delivered the product or services to the client as per the contract and as intended at the time of sale.

3. **Is there a gap?**
   If you believe you have met the contractual obligations and deliverables, then you need to understand where the gap is between what was promised against what has been delivered so far. To do this, you must look at it from the client's point of view so you can see what they are upset about. Your objective is to find out what they are actually complaining about.

   Understanding the gap is critical. The sooner you do, the sooner you can work out if the client's expectations are fair, unreasonable or incorrect. You must determine what the client signed up for against what their expectations were.

4. **What is the business impact?**

   This question relates to the commercial implication of what has gone wrong for the client.

   It is important to stand in the client's shoes, and to do that you need to understand how their business has been affected. The truth is that only when you really grasp the business impact for your client, are you in a position to understand why they are dissatisfied enough to have formally complained or raised an escalation.

5. **What is your/your company's exposure or commercial risk?**

   The last point is to understand your company's exposure or commercial risk. Again, you can only do this once you have a clear understanding of the facts and, based on these, can determine which party may actually have failed to deliver, or simply failed to meet expectations.

   Exposure relates to the extent to which your company contributed or is found to have been responsible. After going through the fact-gathering exercise, I often find that the truth 'falls out' and the facts speak for themselves. In other words, the truth becomes obvious, and from that you can focus on validating what you believe happened.

   Once you have established the exposure or risk to your company, this needs to be factored into your approach to resolving the situation. There are a few different considerations here. It depends on whether the project or engagement is still ongoing, or if you are dealing with a complaint after the fact.

   If a project is still being delivered and the problems identified are during the delivery of services, then resolving the situation may simply require changing current practices or rejigging a process. It may sometimes require a more drastic decision to remove one or more personnel, where certain individuals have been identified as part of the problem or the client has simply lost confidence in them.

However if you need to resolve the situation after the fact, when a project has already failed or been completed but not to the client's satisfaction, then the resolution may require negotiating a financial settlement. Once you know the exposure, you/your company can work out the quantum of money you may need to offer to resolve the dispute.

Let's summarise

This chapter shows the importance of using the facts as the foundation on which to build your position and determine the strength of your argument.

You need to determine what is the truth, and to do that you must follow a structured process that will lead you to the right outcome – a fact-based approach that will give you a clear understanding of what actually happened.

You gather the facts through a series of interviews with up to three people from each of the parties involved in the process. You are seeking answers to the five key questions that will give you the complete story on which to base the resolution process.

Part 2

How to avoid commercial escalations

A commercial escalation is different from any other type of escalation: for example, a technical, product, or project escalation.

A **technical escalation** may be when a product or solution is not working as expected and the problem needs to be addressed by the product development team. It is often related to broken functionality and needs to go through a technical or product development process to resolve.

A **project escalation** may be related to project governance or the methodology used when delivering a project. Therefore it's a complaint about how the project is being or has been run that has led to problems and an escalation.

A **commercial escalation** is always the end result of these other escalations and relates to things that have gone wrong on a project or engagement. It may be the result of a technical, project or non-commercial issue that hasn't been resolved appropriately or quickly enough, or a problem that can't be resolved.

In other words, the broken functionality could not be fixed despite great efforts to do so, or the way in which the project was run or managed was problematic, which created issues that had a broader impact and led to financial implications.

Once the underlying cause has been dealt with, and hopefully resolved as best as possible, the commercial escalation is the fallout your client is left with along with the commercial impact.

Here is how I define a commercial escalation:

- A risk to the commercial relationship between your company and the client, or to the project being delivered
- A breakdown in the relationship that may jeopardise any current or future sales opportunities

- A query as to whether your company delivered to the terms and conditions of the contract
- A threat of legal action.

To be a commercial escalation there must be a contract for an engagement or project, services performed by your company and commercial implications as a result of the issues raised.

When you are asked to get involved in managing an escalation, your role is to understand the challenges, work through the concerns of all parties, and facilitate discussion to achieve agreed outcomes. What I look to achieve is a fair and reasonable outcome for both parties.

This is a very simple philosophy and approach that I highly recommend.

The term 'fair and reasonable' is one that I use regularly throughout the book, just as I do in my job mediating commercial disputes.

Fair and reasonable means we are aiming to achieve an outcome that doesn't favour one party over another. We don't want either party feeling cheated, unfairly treated or not listened to.

Mediators will tell you that a good outcome is where one party feels they could have received more, while at the same time the other party feels they gave away too much. In my view, when both parties walk away and neither party is overly happy, but nonetheless the situation has been resolved, this is a fair and reasonable outcome.

The four-step approach to start a new investigation

Let's assume that you have been asked to get involved in an escalation. It is a situation that has been problematic for a while with various 'blow ups' and you have been asked to sort it out. You can resolve it, but first you need to find out what has happened. This is no different to the job that I do, and in fact why I am engaged. No preparation, no warning, straight into the fire!

Let me explain my four-step approach to starting a new investigation:

Step 1: Understand the issues that have been escalated
As I wrote earlier, you need the facts and a clear understanding of what the client is complaining about.

Step 2: Engage with the existing team
In most situations you don't have the luxury of bringing in your own team, so it makes sense to work with your company's existing project team already on the ground working with the client.

Your objective is to get information as quickly as possible and start to work out what's gone wrong, why and how you can fix it. Who better to start with than those already working on the project who will be able to give you those details - what happened, how the situation unfolded, who did what, when and how?

Step 3: Consider the challenges and obstacles
There are always external factors, and things often don't go to plan or script. These are what I consider the challenges and obstacles

a client may have blamed your company for, without in fact being aware of what really happened.

For example, if there were tasks assigned to the client that were not completed on time, or the client didn't have the appropriately skilled resources, or in fact they didn't have any available resources, the impact may be a major delay to the project that your company has been blamed for. The same scenario often happens when a third-party provider also fails to complete their tasks on time.

Your role is to dig, and find what challenges and obstacles existed and their impact on the project. You need to dive deep into each and understand it completely to make sure that everything is included and presented to the client to give a balanced view of what actually happened. Very often I find these situations have not been discussed with any C-level executives, as people very often try to hide them away or cover them up.

It is extremely important when gathering the facts that you understand all external factors that may have impacted your company's ability to deliver the project based on the contract.

Step 4: Put in place an action plan
Whenever I am brought into any situation, the questions I am asked the most frequently are: What are you going to do? What is your action plan? When will you get started? What will you do to sort this out?

People are eager to see that you have not only taken control, but you have a plan, because that plan gives them confidence. Until they can see that plan clearly set out, they can, and very often do, transfer their nervousness and anxiety to others.

It is essential that when you step in to resolve any problem, you remain composed, patient and calm down the people around you. Give them an idea of your plans by explaining the steps you are taking, the process you will follow and the time you need before they will see any changes. This is already an action plan - the first version – and, more importantly what you are doing is keeping them informed and setting expectations.

Give them an indication of how long steps 1 to 3 will take, and how long you need to come up with an action plan. In that plan, you set out how you intend to resolve the situation. As soon as you've explained that initial action plan, you need agreement from all stakeholders and then you can start to take control.

People and companies delivering IT projects always talk about adopting 'best' practice, and I've often wondered who determines the global standard that makes it best? And how do you know when it is best and not just good enough?

After many years of resolving disputes, I assess situations quite quickly and I am able to separate those projects and companies that deliver 'good enough' practice versus best practice. The difference between them comes down to attention to detail and relates directly to these three key areas.

- Documentation
- Communication
- Accountability.

Also known as DCA.

This is an important concept: I am talking about the attention to detail that a project team gives to what and how they document, the strength of communication between the project team, client, stakeholders and executive sponsors, and the level of accountability shown by the team in terms of making promises, keeping them and delivering to expectations.

From my experience, these three factors – the DCA - are critical to the success or failure of a project.

The hallmarks of all successful projects are a greater attention to detail in the quality of documentation, and the levels of communication and commitment to being fully accountable. Quite simply, if a team fails in any of these areas, it is more likely that the project will fail or create problems that may lead to an escalation, dispute or eventual failure.

Let's dig deeper into each of these critical factors.

Documentation

Documentation is a critical factor in daily, run-of-the-mill project and engagement management. However, it becomes even more important when we rely upon documentation to address complaints, disputes and escalations.

As I've said already, my dispute resolution work is based on the fundamental principle of a fact-based approach. What are the facts? What actually happened? This can't be based on an opinion or someone's version of what they think happened. It needs to be the truth based solely on the facts.

What is written forms the most critical evidence to support discussions, decisions and actions that have been agreed upon.

Documentation comes in a few different forms — what I like to refer as formal or informal.

Formal documentation is when the format by default is already based on what is written. For example, official minutes taken from a meeting or your own set of meeting notes, and emails exchanged between parties.

All of these are in writing and can be relied upon to track a discussion, decision or action. They are the simplest and most straightforward method to track any conversation.

Informal forums such as conversations over coffee, hallway chats, messaging via apps and even walking meetings are a growing trend.

The water cooler conversation is a thing of the past and has turned into meetings that are no longer in the office or at a desk, which means more decisions are being made where there are no notes, no emails and no minutes – just conversation.

So what do you do when this happens? How do you record what was discussed? What was agreed to? Who are the parties involved? And what decisions were made?

I am often asked "So where is the problem?"

Let's fast forward a few weeks or months when something may have gone wrong with a project. People are asking questions, and they pinpoint the time to when a decision was made, or an action was taken.

What do you do when someone determines that the decision was made over a coffee, and you have no notes or details documented of what was discussed in that conversation? While you may be confident that the problem or action taken was an informed one, agreed to by the client, where do you have that proof in writing?

Worse still, what happens if one of the key people who was involved in that decision has left the company and is no longer around to back you up and confirm that the conversation took place?

Or what if the decision-maker is replaced by someone new who comes on board and starts to ask questions about the problems they have inherited? They will want to look into how the problems arose.

Your actions and decisions will be under scrutiny. They consider that a critical decision was made, and they ask you when this was discussed. Who was consulted? Who agreed to it? And the big one...where is it documented?

Best practice means the standard of your working practices always ensures that there is evidence to support all decisions, including details of what was discussed, what was agreed, the people involved and the basis on which to proceed.

Documentation is a critical element in adopting a best practice approach. Whether you are the program director, project manager, specialist consultant or administrative support – every member of the project team has a role to play in adopting best practice standards.

Documentation can be managed in the most basic form, so there is no excuse for not making a commitment to your documentation. A simple approach would be writing things down, recording them and emailing them so they can be saved in the official project tool records. A more structured approach is adopting the tools that your project manager is using and recording all your notes directly as part of the overall project methodology.

On the subject of informal meeting forums: making a note and filing it away is not really sufficient to protect yourself. After every informal meeting, I always recommend that as a standard practice you send an email to the other party detailing what was discussed, what was agreed to and the actions stemming from that conversation. I also suggest that you copy other interested parties, including a decision-maker who is most likely to be your project manager,

You should request an email reply agreeing that you are aligned, that what you have documented is accurate, and confirming their approval to go ahead.

People often tell me that they can send an email, but what happens if the client doesn't reply? Just write in your email that you will not be able to start until you have that confirmation email. Make it simple for them by indicating that all they need it to say is 'yes', 'approved' or 'agreed'. It doesn't need any more.

And lastly, if you still have not received a response after sending a reminder or two, there is no harm in picking up the phone and calling your colleague. You only need to say, "I sent you an email that needs your response in writing before I can do anything."

You must remain firm that you need it in writing, as people often tell you that you are aligned over the phone and think this is enough. Of course, it's not enough for you, because you need the response in writing. Explaining that you can't get started until you have that email will force them to send it because they want the work to start.

I've yet to see any situation where, after following this practice, a client has not responded.

 **TIP**

Sample email to send after an informal meeting

"Hi Dave,

Thanks again for the coffee this morning. Just a quick note to confirm that, as discussed, we agree to proceed with...

1. Etc.. etc.
2. Etc.. etc.

If you can please reply with a brief email confirming that we are aligned, it would be greatly appreciated. I will need to have this in writing before I can get started.

Please let me know if there are any queries or concerns.

Regards,"

Best practice is all about processes that ensure you are well prepared for circumstances that are not ideal. The ideal scenario is when a topic is discussed in a meeting and there are formal minutes. However, you can't assume or rely on ideals.

The important tips are:

- Make documentation a part of your best practice regime.

- Be fastidious about capturing important moments in writing, even if they are only your notes recording what happened, with no reason to share with anyone else.

- In particular, have a system for capturing documentation for non-formal or informal forums as these are usually the ones that come unstuck when it matters.

Always be ready for someone like me coming along and asking for proof to support your version of the truth. Then it's never a question of whether you have it documented.

There is no excuse for not making a commitment to your documentation.

Communication

Poor communication is almost always a major reason why projects fail.

This is not just for technology projects but for projects across all industries. If you think about it, it should be obvious. Program directors, project managers and team leaders who don't manage their teams well, who don't keep stakeholders informed and who fail to prioritise communication are more likely to deliver sub-standard projects and poor outcomes.

Why? Because they invariably fail to keep people up to date on key issues as they arise. They struggle to keep their teams aligned and in-sync, and they don't notify their stakeholders and executive sponsors of potential major problems on a timely basis.

Delivery people, by their nature alone, tend to prefer to keep issues quiet while they try to sort them out themselves. The fact that they commonly don't report information when they should is in itself a sign that there is a problem.

In the previous section, Documentation, I pointed out that best practice requires attention to detail. People who are strong communicators tend to pay attention to detail. They are on top of what is happening, and they have processes in place to make sure that they are the first to know of a challenge before it becomes a problem; they are efficient and they pride themselves on keeping others informed.

Can you communicate too much? Yes, you definitely can over-communicate by sending too many emails and providing too many updates too often - and to the same people. However, over-communicating is actually much less of a problem than under-communicating.

I want you to think about your own job and responsibilities, irrespective of whether you are in sales, services or management, and ask:

1. Do you communicate enough?
2. Do the people on your team, or in your reporting line receive clear and regular communication from you on the status of a project or an engagement?
3. Do your internal stakeholders (i.e your company's internal senior/executive management) know enough about the key issues affecting the project or engagement that you manage?
4. Are the client's key stakeholders — that is the C-level executives, executive sponsors and financial controller — aware of the challenges and risks to their project?
5. Do they know what may be going wrong and what they are ultimately responsible for fixing?
6. If there are any external third-party stakeholders, are they being kept informed of what is going on?

The reality is that communication at the level needed to ensure success, does not occur anywhere near enough.

Being great at communication is actually very hard work, but critical for success. Most managers will be honest enough to tell you that they do a good job, but not a great job, of keeping people informed. Strong communicators make it a priority to keep all parties informed of what is happening, any challenges, and which decisions require their input. They do this regularly and whenever appropriate, and they usually update people on the project before they have to be asked.

So what can you change today to make you a better communicator?

We all want to deliver best practice, but all too often fall short of the mark. Here are some important tips on what you can change now that will help you be a better communicator.

Failure to communicate is not an option

Consider this scenario: you promise a client an update by a certain time, however it is reliant on someone else giving you an answer first. What do you do if you still have not received that information by that deadline?

Do you decide not to contact your client because you have nothing to tell them? Or do you contact them and say you don't have any new information for them?

The typical mistake that so many people make is the decision not to communicate at all because you have nothing new to say. Whilst this might be easier for you to avoid the awkwardness of telling them something they don't want to hear, it is not the smartest approach. Leaving your client wondering why you haven't called is more likely to make them feel that you forgot. Which is far from the real reason, which is that you had not forgotten them, but you had nothing to tell them. And, especially in a situation that may be on the verge of an escalation, you can't afford to make things worse.

The smart move is to accept that you are going to disappoint them and to be prepared for an awkward conversation. You should be upfront and explain that the information has not yet come through, and you are calling to let them know that you don't have an update, but you didn't want them to think you had forgotten.

Imagine if the deadline you set was a Friday and you chose not to contact your client to let them know the status or lack of it. The client goes home agitated that you were not in touch when you said you would be, and spends all weekend stewing. On Monday morning they send you an angry email asking why they haven't heard from you and saying how disappointed they are.

The alternative scenario is that it's Friday, the deadline is looming, you still have no information and you know you will not get it by the end of the day. You make a better decision, which is to call your client, or send them an email saying that your colleague has not come through with the information, but you wanted to let them know so they don't think you've forgotten them. Then you reset their expectations and tell them when you will provide the information.

Your client will go home that night understanding that you don't have the answers they expected, but understand why and, most importantly, that you hadn't forgotten them. On Monday, you won't be dealing with an angry client, as they will appreciate the fact you kept them informed. As long as you meet the reset expectation, your client and the relationship will be unaffected.

It is extremely important that you constantly set, reassess and reset expectations if they can't be met based on the original plan.

Don't wait to share bad news

While no one wants to hear about something that has gone wrong, the reality is that projects rarely go to plan. Did you know that most companies actually plan for a project to have challenges? They factor these into their contingency planning taking into account both time and budget.

The most common reason for keeping bad news quiet is that you are concerned about the disappointment that will be generated and the reaction you will need to deal with internally or from your client. But holding back bad news simply puts more pressure on you and the situation.

Delivery people by their nature tend to keep problems and bad news to themselves for as long as possible. They have a fix-it mentality and believe that they can sort out issues if you just give them more time.

They work on the basis that until they have had a chance to fix it, they prefer no one needs to know. This is not necessarily to be secretive or protective of their reputation: it is sometimes just a matter of pride. But if they can't fix it, they may feel that to some extent they have failed. Of course, the possibility of repercussions may also play on their minds.

The earlier you inform all parties concerned of a bad news story, the sooner they can react, regroup and decide how to minimise the impact or implement damage control.

Holding back on sharing the reality of a situation, especially if it is negative, tends to lead to loss of confidence in you by the client. If not managed carefully, that can grow to a loss of confidence in the entire project management, especially if they see that the problem was not flagged early enough.

Embrace best practice and don't wait to share bad news. Make sure that your communication is clear and concise so that what you say is understood.

As you know, a good manager does not come to you, tell you there is a problem and wait for you to find them a solution. Good managers bring a problem to your attention along with the solution, or at least a number of options and ideas to throw around.

Therefore part of your communication should include a high-level plan, ready with the options and potential actions to be considered. You should always present enough detail, telling people exactly what they need to know. They don't want a report that is the length of a book... keep it short and stick to the main points, especially when communicating at senior and executive levels.

One last point: don't assume that bad news comes as a surprise to anyone senior. Most senior executives expect things to go wrong, and therefore bad news is not always a surprise - the surprise is when nothing goes wrong. Within their plans they have factored in any surprise elements as a contingency component, and they have probably planned for delays or an impact on the budget.

Also, don't take it personally or assume you'll be judged on your failure. Bad news is common in projects. The key is to make sure you learn something from the experience, that will help you in future projects.

Executives don't like surprises

Communicating bad news is the one of the hardest tasks for anyone, at every level of management.

The most common thing an executive will tell you is that they don't like surprises. Your intention should always be to deliver bad news in person or by phone. Although this is extremely challenging, it is almost always the better option and much more appreciated than an email.

I deal with bad news most weeks, and these are my three key rules:

Rule #1 — Protect your executives from finding out about a problem situation or bad news on a project from other people. It's worse still if they hear it from the client first. There is no worse surprise for an executive than to walk into a client meeting and hear something has gone wrong when you should have warned them first.

A strong communicator will always make sure to give any bad news to their executives, so that they don't hear it from anyone else first.

Rule #2 – Protect the confidence and trust that others have in your abilities to manage problems or a crisis. As a strong communicator you must ensure that your executives maintain full confidence and trust in your ability to manage. This is easily lost if they hear about a problem from someone else when they expected you to brief them first. Therefore, you must make sure that they are never the last to know.

The way in which you deal with problem situations is a chance to impress your senior leaders with your management style and show your ability to take the lead. In every situation I consider who needs to know the bad news before they hear it from someone else.

Rule #3 — Be prepared by thinking through how you are going to deliver the news and how you are going to respond. Being defensive or fearful won't help you resolve an issue.

 **TIP**

Sample email for communicating bad news

If you fear giving senior people bad news and getting a negative reaction, then you are not alone.

You most definitely want to try and tell people any bad news in person or by phone. I do not recommend you just send an email and hope for the best. You need to know that they have received the news, understood it and not blown it out of proportion, which is why having a conversation of some sort always gives you the chance to make sure nothing has been misinterpreted.

Most people fear giving bad news because of the reaction. You can soften the impact of the initial conversation by sending a gentle heads-up email first, alluding to the problem.

Your email would go something like this:

"I would appreciate seeing you to discuss a problem I have just identified.

Due to an issue with……the project is going to require …… which may lead to a further delay in the date we can go live.

> *If you would please let me know when you have 30 minutes free for us to discuss this, I will explain in more detail."*

As you can see, if you do this in an initial email, the element of surprise is removed. What is very important is that, in the same communication, you say you want to meet with them face to face to discuss the problem.

This way you achieve your objective of flagging that there is bad news without explaining. You have avoided the element of surprise and having to deal with their initial reaction face to face.

When crafting an email, less is more

"If you can't explain it simply, you don't understand it well enough." Albert Einstein.

How and what you write in your communications are extremely important. How and what you write should make it as easy as possible for your audience to understand the points and not get lost in the words.

I believe that writing is an artform and I prefer to use the term 'crafting' an email. Choosing the right words, the appropriate tone, and picking the best format to deliver the message are all critical aspects of communication.

You need to be efficient. Use fewer words to make your point and avoid repeating yourself. If you get your message right in the first line, you shouldn't need to repeat it in the next line. A short, succinct email works much better than a wordy one.

Consider your audience is the key to best practice. It is important for you to stand in their shoes and think about what they need to know. Decide what they may want to ask you and then make sure that your briefing addresses all of those questions. It makes your communication even more effective when there is nothing left for them to ask.

For example, if you are sending an email to executives, just give the key points they need. They don't need to know the project level detail, so don't include it because that only confuses your message.

If you are sending an email to update your project team, then your communication should provide the more detailed, granular, information that they need. The point here is to always tailor your communication to the specific audience.

The most common mistake people make is to send out one general communication to everyone, with all details to all parties. This is often going to confuse the message because, in a broad group, some will not need that level of detail and wonder why you have included it.

To avoid that issue, if you want to send the update on one email, make sure that your format presents the executive summary and relevant information in the top section of the email. Then separately have the detail in the bottom section for anyone interested to read on.

If you are asking executives or stakeholders to make critical decisions on a particular issue, then consider what they need to know. Including that in your email it will make their decision a lot easier.

 **TIP**

What should be included in an executive briefing?

If you are writing executive briefings or updates, try to keep them to one page. A structure you may want to use includes three key headings:

- Current status
- Next steps
- Background

Current status should provide the key points of where a project is at, informing the reader of the main challenges: you should also state who is managing the situation, so it is clear who is the go-to person.

Next steps should show you have got this covered, you have an action plan, and the right people are engaged. Share the plan, outlining who is doing what and when. This will give all stakeholders, (yours and your client) the confidence that you know what to do next. You should also state when they can expect your next update.

Background should be put at the back of the briefing pack, for anyone who needs to be brought up to speed on the key information regarding the project or engagement, so a conversation is not necessary to update them. Why put it at the back when people need to read this first? Because once they have read it, they won't need to read it again and can focus on the current status and next steps. Having the background at the end keeps it out of the way of ongoing updates, but there for anyone needing to reference it.

The background should describe the project and provide some history. It should tell the reader enough for them not to need to ask anything more, and when they next read the current status it will make sense.

Make sure your sentences are clear and that your words cannot be misinterpreted. Avoid any ambiguous statements that may cause confusion.

Don't forget to pick up the phone

Strong communicators will meet people in person and pick up the phone to talk to their stakeholders and team members regularly. Poor communicators will email everything and where possible avoid talking to anyone.

Although documenting and putting things in writing is a critical aspect of best practice, that should not overshadow the importance of talking to people. Documenting and talking: you can -and need to do both.

When it comes to avoiding escalations, don't rely on email as your only form of communication. Very often people fall into the trap of sending an email that needs an urgent response and when they haven't had a response, they follow up with another. I have known many situations where this has happened, and when I ask the person for an update and their response is "I haven't heard back," I then ask, "What did they say when you called them?" and they often say they haven't called.

The phone is still the most effective form of direct communication. When you need to, pick it up and speak to someone.

Accountability

When it comes to being accountable, the words I never want to hear someone say about me are "he is no different to all the others". Put simply, accountability is all about being accountable, answerable and responsible for the promises you make and the actions you sign up for. Don't make promises for anything you can't deliver.

You will have noticed that the three elements of best practice all tie in very closely with one another:

Documentation is committing to writing what you plan to do or have done. **Communication** is all about telling people and groups what they need to know on a timely basis.

Accountability is all about doing what you have said you will do. There is nothing worse than someone who takes on a set of actions or makes promises and then doesn't deliver on them. This is a credibility killer! Failing to deliver immediately puts your character into question, and once you lose trust, you've lost the confidence and respect of the other party.

When managing disputes and escalations, clients will often tell me about the people who were involved before me and who made promises they did not keep. There is a golden rule for escalated situations: you don't want to be labelled or seen in the same light as anyone else who has failed to deliver on their promise. Every day I remind myself of this.

When I present myself to clients as the person responsible to fix a situation, I am aware that other people may have made exactly the same promises. For whatever reasons, my predecessors could not deliver. If I can't either, then I shall be seen as yet another person who promised to solve everything and fixed nothing. And they will kick me out!

My three key 'accountability' rules:

1. **Never commit to anything that you can't deliver** or if you think there is a chance that you can't deliver.

    Be very careful how you word any commitments. For example, rather than saying "I will have this sorted out for you this week, leave it to me", I would say "I can't promise when this will happen, but let me see if I can get something in place by the end of this week. I will let you know how it goes", or words to that effect.

2. **Communicate changes to commitments sooner rather than later.** In the event that you make a commitment to do something only to find that it won't be done in time, inform people as soon as you know so they can change their plans if necessary.

People appreciate being kept informed and will be happier knowing that, even though things have changed, you have told them on a timely basis.

3. **Setting expectations is a very important action** - but resetting them is even more important. This doesn't only apply to problem situations and escalations, but to all actions and situations.

    Setting expectations creates a level of certainty and confidence where people can make other decisions and, while it may seem obvious, I find that not everyone does this as a part of their everyday best practice. Resetting expectations is even more crucial because it shows you can remain agile and flexible when things don't go to plan. Creating a new set of expectations shows authority, leadership and strong management.

Accountability is about being responsible for what you promise and making sure you follow though until completion. Steps you should take to remain accountable include;

1. Document the commitments made
2. Take the actions needed to meet expectations with plenty of time before the deadline.
3. Assess how you're tracking to deliver the promises made, and inform the client should their expectations need to change
4. Communicate regularly, especially where there are changes to a plan, and make sure you update everyone who needs to know.

Delivering best practice is hard work. It requires attention to detail, high energy and a commitment to maintain the highest standards, not just some of the time but all of the time. When you do it right, your results and reputation are worth the effort.

Let's summarise

The three key elements that are critical to avoiding commercial escalations are documentation, communication and accountability.

In order to deliver successful projects and engagements, you must set the highest standard and adopt best practice in each of these three areas. They are not only key ingredients to success, but equally key factors of failure.

You need to:

1. Document all critical information so you can rely upon it when necessary.
2. Communicate regularly with your stakeholders, your teams and all interested parties, and keep them all informed. Tailor your communications to your audience.
3. Make sure you keep all interested parties informed of the critical issues and details; be accountable at all times for the promises you make to maintain the trust, confidence and credibility you want people to have in you.
4. Set high standards and be accountable for the quality and delivery of your work. Do what you say you will in the timeframe, and by the deadlines you set.

5. Adhere to standards and practices from a team perspective and set standards that everyone can achieve. Adopt these as best practices.
6. Everyone has a role to play in adopting and committing to best practices. You can't be involved in every conversation, discussion and decision that takes place, but you can set a standard to ensure that everyone keeps records and commits to the three critical factors above to give you, your team and your project the best chance of success.

Part 3

How to manage commercial escalations (when it's too late to avoid)

Up to now, I have shared the best practices to be adopted in order to avoid causing commercial escalations.

Obviously, every organisation prefers to avoid escalations by applying the highest standards and best practices. The rest of the book focuses on ways and techniques to manage commercial escalations. This assumes that you have a situation where an escalation could not be avoided and you now need the expertise to deal with it.

Let's work on the following scenario - your project or engagement is on fire and, despite your company's best efforts, your client is unhappy and the situation has gone into escalation. It is now up to you to manage things.

In this section of the book, I will share how I have approached typical escalations like this and resolved them with great success, focusing on three important elements:

- The relationship — how to manage your relationship with the client
- The approach — how to structure an approach to resolve the issues that have gone wrong, and in particular address fallout and damage control
- The negotiation — how to negotiate to get the outcome you set out to achieve.

When managing an escalation, your first priority is to understand your **relationship** with your client and how to manage it in a sensitive situation. Then comes the **approach** and all the factors that dictate setting up the handling of an escalation for a successful outcome. The third and final element is the **negotiation**, and the ways in to achieve the desired outcome.

One thing I want to mention upfront is that people often think that resolving an escalation is not complicated and doesn't need much planning, just an ability to wing it and see how it goes. I can tell you from experience that without a well-thought-out strategy and careful execution, your negotiation will fail.

The process to manage an escalation is similar to the sales process. Anyone in sales knows how hard it is to get a contract signed. Managing an escalation is much the same, but more difficult because you don't have a willing client. Instead, the client is upset, angry and disappointed about an outcome that is not what they signed up for.

Given the sensitivities needed to manage the client and still achieve a successful outcome, the odds are already stacked against you. However if you follow my technique and approach, you will transform every unhappy client into a satisfied one, and turn an escalation situation into a real success.

Done well, you can enjoy a relationship with your client that may last a long time.

When I talk about the negotiation, I'm not referring to finances, contract or compensation. What I mean is how to negotiate with a client to achieve the desired outcome in any difficult situation.

The point is to understand that every client meeting is a negotiation. That means in each and every meeting with your client, you need to consider the outcome you want, the strategy needed to achieve that and the approach you will take to do so. In other words, while you must have a big picture outcome in mind that you set out to achieve, each individual meeting contributes to the 'one step at a time' approach towards overall resolution.

In an escalation situation, protecting the relationship is the first step. When things go wrong, the first thing any client will do is watch how you and your company respond. There is you as an individual, as a person, as a professional and as a trusted advisor. The client wants to see how you will look after them in a time of crisis.

Equally, they will be looking at your organisation and how it responds in such a situation. As we know, companies are always there for you when there is a sales opportunity, but the true test of a relationship is when things go wrong.

The Relationship

Trust – it takes years to gain, but just one wrong move to lose

"It takes twenty years to build a reputation and five minutes to ruin it. If you think about that, you'll do things differently." Warren Buffet.

We spend years building relationships, nurturing them, and doing all the right things to keep our clients happy, to keep them coming back again and again. We think after years of positive engagement that our client relationships are strong and can withstand any problem situation.

But trust is a really interesting emotion and it only takes one thing to go wrong, one false move for all that goodwill and trust to be gone.

Clients are tough judges when assessing how an organisation handles their problem situation, and will always measure their true worth to an organisation based on how they are treated in difficult situations. This is irrespective of the trust you thought had been built up in your relationship with them.

Clients expect that when something has gone wrong, the organisation will be there to support them and stand behind the loyalty they have shown as a client. They judge the relationship based on our behaviour on two levels:

The first is who you are as a person, on an individual level as their trusted advisor, the person with whom they feel that they have built up a trusted relationship over a period of time.

The second is on an organisational level, where they judge how the company behaves. They assess how genuine the company is in putting the client first, over and above itself. In escalation situations, many companies 'go missing' and react poorly to any suggestion of wrongdoing, often refusing to accept criticism for what may have happened.

Good companies are prepared to acknowledge problems, accept a level of responsibility and work through the issues until they are amicably resolved. Most importantly, they have a process that they revert to in such situations, and they are transparent in the way they achieve the outcome. Not-so-good companies are defensive and quick to point the finger, refusing to acknowledge any part they have played in the problem.

The true test of a good client relationship is not when things are going right, but when they go wrong. Behaviour is critically important, however this doesn't mean giving in to the client's demands irrespective of who is right and who is wrong. It requires a balanced assessment of the situation, understanding where the problem started and, most importantly, how you are going to resolve it in a fair and reasonable way.

When you are in any problem situation you must **listen, take action and be accountable.** In problem times you must **communicate more,** not less, and this is the time when you should **show leadership** and **take ownership.**

The first step in dealing with an escalation is to bring together what I will call 'the relationship team'. These are all the people who have relationships with the client, and who must work together for you to be successful. It is extremely important that you don't do this on your own: the team has to form part of your approach. You don't need, for example, an account executive deciding to take ownership of resolving the situation, as well as the delivery executive. Two individuals trying to achieve the same outcome will cause contradiction and duplication of effort, which is more than enough to frustrate the client even more and drive them further away.

As part of the overall strategy and approach to any dispute situation, you need to sort out who should be involved, the roles each will play and, most importantly, who will lead the escalation. You must make sure that you are all aligned and working together to protect the client relationship.

In an escalation, the team must agree that only one person assumes control, and everyone follows their lead. It is disastrous when one person is given the lead and someone else decides to take matters into their own hands. If you undermine your leader, you are working against each other and making resolution much harder than it already is.

It's also important that, when things become problematic, you don't run away or hide just because you're not good at dealing with confrontation, escalations or disappointment. A true leader and a person with strong relationships will be forthright in maintaining contact with the client, remain focused on looking after them, reassuring them that you have their best interests at heart and that you will see this through with them. It's important that you lean on your strengths and the strength of your relationship when it is needed most, and it is this approach that will hold you in good stead in protecting a trusted relationship.

Consider how you have handled escalations in the past: when situations have become problematic, did you run away or throw yourself at it?

 **TIP**

What to do first when you get involved in an escalation

Here are some tips to keep in mind when you first get involved in a dispute or an escalation.

1. Before you speak to your customer, ensure you have a good initial briefing from colleagues involved in the project or engagement.

2. Map out an internal communication strategy to manage any damage or fallout. Share it with all key internal stakeholders so everyone is aligned.

3. Aim to make every customer interaction a positive experience.

4. Arrange to meet the customer, ideally face to face. If you are working under COVID restrictions, make it a conference call with cameras turned on.

5. Explain that the purpose of the first meeting is to listen to them, and you are not coming with the answers.

6. Find out as much as possible beforehand about who you are meeting, their character and personality type.

7. Show empathy.

8. Confirm your commitment to working with your client, so they know you will remain engaged until the situation is resolved.

9. Use language such as 'we' and 'I' to personalise your communication.

10. Make sure you consult with your legal advisers and stakeholder management team before making any commitments. Never make promises you can't keep.

How do you handle unhappy clients?

One of the biggest problems I find when a situation has escalated is that the client has not had the opportunity to get everything off their chest. More often than not they feel that they haven't been listened to. Until they have told their side of the story, said everything they need to and given you what they consider is the full picture from their perspective, it will be hard to progress.

The first step in managing an unhappy client is to arrange a meeting, and then let them do all the talking.

The meeting place is not overly important, and I would only suggest you make sure it is where the client feels most comfortable, and you need to be okay with the location too. My personal preference is to meet at the client's offices, and you can offer that up as a suggestion, but ultimately let them make the decision. It needs to be somewhere they feel they can speak their mind. They may want to get loud or be somewhere private, which means a café normally wouldn't work.

The only reason I have not suggested your workplace is that the client may feel they are not in a familiar environment that allows them to open up as they would like. Remember, your objective is to encourage them to talk openly and honestly, so you don't want to compromise the opportunity.

Arrange the meeting, and make sure they know that its purpose is for you to understand their concerns and listen to their story. Explain that you are not coming with answers, but they should talk, share their views on what happened and spell out how it came to this.

Don't underestimate the fact that listening when you're feeling under threat or being criticised is a challenge. You have to resist the urge to interrupt, defend yourself or get emotional.

Your body language is an important part of this. It should be relaxed but open. No folded arms or sitting back in your chair as if you don't really care.

Just a quick recommendation on body language - I was once given a fascinating tip which I find works very well: the experts say when meeting someone one-on-one, you should always mimic the body language of the other person to show you are aligned.

In other words, if they sit back in a relaxed manner in their chair, you should too (although not too relaxed). If they sit upright or lean forward and are attentive then you should do the same.

Of course, you need to be careful as you don't want to be seen copying their every move, however be subtle and aware of what they are doing. Obviously, you still make sure you feel comfortable as that comes first. And if they get up and start to walk around, don't follow them around the room.

Overall, you want your body language to show that you are caring, empathetic and attentive.

In escalation meetings, I find the trick to staying positive, and remaining calm and unemotional is all about your state of mind. If you approach a meeting expecting criticism, ready to listen and not needing to provide answers, you will stay calm. If you are worried about what they may say, if they'll get angry and will you have answers, then you will be on edge from the beginning.

My approach is to think, how bad can it get? I know they are going to get upset, they are going to be critical and maybe slightly abusive towards the company. If you go into the meeting knowing this, then whatever happens you won't be caught by surprise.

If the client knows that you are not coming with answers, but only to listen, it immediately takes the pressure off you. Besides, it also makes sense. How can you possibly provide answers on what went wrong and how you're going to fix the situation when you don't yet know from the client's perspective exactly what they are upset about.

You need to have the first meeting and let the client explain their complaint. If you try to fix a problem before you know all the details, you will inevitably come to the wrong conclusion and most likely make promises you should not have made. When you do this, you're accepting the blame for things that happened simply because you believed everything you were told, without having the process to question and clarify what really happened.

In financial terms it is most likely you will settle the situation for a lot more money than you should.

The first meeting

When you attend the first meeting, always take a friendly approach and don't assume you are walking into a firestorm. Of course, you may well be, but don't take it for granted. Start the meeting by thanking them for giving you the time to properly investigate the escalation they have raised. Outline your approach and, in particular, explain to them that your company has a defined process in situations like these for managing disputes and escalations. You don't need to go into the details, but the fact that you have said that there is a process often gives the client a great deal of comfort that the situation will be well handled.

Next is to ask the client to tell you what happened from their perspective. It is really important that you don't interrupt when they tell their story. Encourage them to tell you everything, because that will take a lot of the heat out of the situation.

In my early years, I would sit in on meetings run by one of my company's executives who would ask the client for their version of the story. Then someone else at the table would interrupt when they didn't agree with the facts and say 'No, that's not what happened actually. Let me tell you what happened.' A discussion would ensue, and the client would lose their flow and the opportunity to talk freely.

So I learnt that one person needed to control the meeting to prevent this from happening. I became that person, and today I run these meetings one-to-one to ensure there are no interruptions in that crucial first meeting. You must always avoid interrupting a client because it stops them from telling their story from their perspective and getting it off their chest.

My second tip is you must take notes so that you have the details of the pain points that the client has experienced.

If the engagement or project is still in progress (in other words, if the escalation is not after the fact), then you have the opportunity to make some changes and fix the things that have upset the client. Taking notes means you have something written to refer to. Without notes, you will miss some points, which can only make matters worse.

Make sure the client knows that you are taking notes and does not think you are doodling or bored. In relation to body language, taking notes shows your attention to detail and that you are taking the client seriously. It is also impressive when you meet them several weeks later to be able to run through each of the points and explain what actions you have already taken to address them.

With a project that is still in progress, the more pain you can take away by acting quickly, the sooner you will be able to calm things down and get the situation back to normal. However, if the project in escalation is already finished and has either failed or was simply a poor experience for the client, then the notes you take are a key part of the fact-gathering process .

The first meeting is the initial step in the fact-gathering process and your first opportunity to listen and start understanding what actually happened. Remember that if you don't really know their problems, what and how they feel, the pressure they are under and the implications for them and their company, then you won't know where to start to help resolve them.

I've seen many situations where the account executive or delivery manager was brought in to help fix a problem only to find that they made assumptions without enough fact-based evidence, leading them to try and fix the wrong problem, because they didn't take the time to find out exactly what the client's pain points were.

The process for gathering the facts

Putting the full story together before jumping in allows you to understand what needs to be fixed and in what order. It stops you from going down the wrong path and further agitating the client, making them question why you did that and who will pay.

To pull together the full story, you need answers to the following seven questions:

What actually happened?
What did your company do or not do?
What did the client do or not do?
Was there a third-party involved and, if so, what did they do or not do?
What are the allegations against your company?
What is their claim against you?
What does the client want as the resolution: action, money or both?

Stay focused on getting the answers to these questions as they will help you zero in on what matters. By asking each of the people whom you are relying upon for the facts, you will find out very quickly what actually happened, which parties were involved in the delivery, who did what and, most importantly, who did not deliver what was expected of them. You will also find out exactly what they are blaming your company for and how they would like the situation resolved.

It is really important that you don't make any assumptions in terms of the answers to these questions, as very often I have found what the client actually wants is either action or financial compensation. Therefore never assume anything, and always ask the question in order to learn the answers.

How do you ensure you get to the truth?

When investigating a dispute, you need the correct version, based on what actually happened and in the right sequence.

The more people you interview, the more versions or variations of 'the truth' you'll hear. Each different party also has different vested interests in the outcome, which can often colour what they recall happened.

Here is the technique I use to ensure that I get to the truth:

Key Steps:

1. Document all the information that you have been given by the various parties in interviews, written documentation and oral communications

2. Separate out each consistent point everyone appears to agree with

3. Identify the facts that don't align – these are the contentious issues you need to investigate further

4. Continue the investigation and interviews until you get a consistent/agreed position from all parties on what actually happened.

The first meeting is with the person who has raised the complaint - usually the CEO, a senior executive, the head of the business unit or the business owner. That is the first person I need to meet as they made the complaint and escalated it. Therefore I first run through a set of questions with them that help me answer the seven questions I listed earlier.

In that first meeting, I explain the process that we will follow, formalising any investigation into the truth.

Following this meeting you should aim to interview two or three people from each of the parties who have been or are involved in the project: from the client's project team, your project team and, if a third-party has been involved, up to three members of their project team.

It is important that you see each of these people one-on-one and not in a group, the reason being that in a group someone will dominate the talking and the others may be influenced, which changes with their own views of what happened. Since you are trying to establish the facts as clearly as possible, the more versions of what happened you can collect, the more chance of inconsistencies will emerge.

You ask each of the individuals you interview the same questions, so if you interview three people from each of three parties you will conduct nine interviews looking for **consistencies** and **inconsistencies** in the facts.

When many or most of the answers that you get are consistent across the group, you know that you are being told the truth. The key is to delve into the inconsistencies: the facts you have been given that are not consistent across the group. This may be where you will find out something more.

The question here is why only one person has raised this point. Why didn't anyone else see what they claim happened? If it is true, then who is telling you the truth?

It is digging into the inconsistencies where you will discover what really happened in a situation, and when you present this to the group, you will most likely uncover what others have either been trying to hide or confirm that this single fact did not actually happen.

This process is crucial to any investigation into an escalation of dispute and, when done properly, it more often than not exposes hidden agendas or people trying to cover their tracks.

So once you've done the first round of interviews, you will have gathered a set of facts. But do they tell the full story? There is the list of facts that are consistent across the board, and you can put these aside as being correct or accurate enough - if most people said it happened, you can accept that's what happened.

What you now need to carry out is a second round of interviews querying any inconsistencies shown. My approach is to question each person again, honing in on the outlier facts – the ones that not everyone agreed on.

our objective is to explore why they didn't raise some of the points and find out whether they actually happened. Why did only one or a few say they happened?

It is important that you don't identify who provided certain answers or any specific information as you need to create a strong feeling of trust between everyone, and understanding that what you are trying to do is identify the truth rather than point the finger of blame.

Sometimes people try to be clever and say something like "I assume it was Simon who told you that." In such a situation, you need to remain impartial, and your response should be "It doesn't matter who said it; I am only interested to know if it did happen. If it did, why didn't you tell me? if it didn't, why do you think the point was made? What do you believe happened in regard to that?"

There have been many situations where I have carried out three rounds of interviews before being satisfied that the facts are all clear and I am comfortable with the conclusions drawn. So don't be surprised and don't let anyone suggest otherwise if you feel that multiple rounds of questions are necessary before you are satisfied that you have all the information you need.

At the end of the interview stage, you will have a set of facts that you can rely on about what happened, and a further set of facts that, while not everyone may agree, where you can see what is most likely to have happened.

Once you are confident that the facts are accurate, then it is important to document and share them with the client. You should present them as the findings of your investigation, representing the facts on which you will base the dispute resolution and form your position.

Now you're ready to start working towards a resolution.

Let's summarise

1. Arrange a meeting with the person who escalated the matter and make it clear to the client that you are there to listen, not to provide answers and not there to suggest ways forward.

2. From this meeting you can create a list of the client's concerns. This shows you their pain points, which means if you focus on addressing those and resolving them to their satisfaction, they will have nothing left to complain about.

3. When you go into these meetings to listen, you are not only creating a positive situation by encouraging the client to get all their problems off their chest, you are also compiling a comprehensive list of issues which once addressed will take away all of the pain. This is extremely powerful in turning unhappy clients into loyal ones.

4. It is critical for you to put the full story together before you start to fix anything. All too often people jump right into solution mode before they have a proper understanding of the problem. Putting the full story together first allows you to see what needs to be fixed and in what order, and stops you going down the wrong path which would not only further agitate the client but make them question why you did that and who is going to pay.

5. To pull together the full story, you need the answers to the following questions (refer point 6 below) which will help you focus and zero in on what really matters to them, not what you think matters to them. Most importantly, this will be an excellent starting point for repairing the relationship.

6. In order to find out what actually happened, you need answers to the following key questions:

    a. What actually happened?

    b. What did your company do or not do in terms of what was agreed in the contract or the project plan?

    c. What did the client do or not do?

    d. What did any third-party do or not do?

    e. What are the allegations against your company?

    f. What is their claim against you?

    g. What does the client want as resolution? Is it action, money or both?

The Approach

At this stage, you have met your client and held your first interview with them. You may even have finished all the interviews.

You have re-established a rapport and relationship and, overall, the situation is moving in the right direction. Now comes the Approach, and all the factors you need to take into account that will make a difference to how you achieve a successful outcome.

The Approach is all about the "how" in our equation: how to achieve the outcome we have set out. The how revolves around the style, personnel and tone we take in the next planned meeting with the client.

Style relates to the way in which we wish to conduct ourselves and the meeting; personnel refers to the people we need on the team who are best placed to help us achieve our objective; tone relates to the mood we wish to create in the room: for example do we want to come across as strong, businesslike and aggressive or shall we take a softer, quieter approach?

More often than not, the heat of the situation and the mood of the client dictate the approach we feel will achieve a positive result.

Strategy + Approach = Outcome

I have a formula for every meeting that I attend for every escalation: Strategy (Plan) + Approach (How) = the Outcome (Result).

In other words, what is the plan and how will you go about executing it to achieve the outcome or result that you want.

I'll refer to this as S+A = O.

Starting with the Outcome, think about a situation you need to resolve and write down the Outcome you want. Then work backwards and think about the Strategy and Approach. By Strategy I mean what topics, items or subjects do you need to put on the table for discussion that relate to the Outcome.

Once you've decided on the Outcome you seek, your Approach relates to how you raise the topics, what you will say and your position on each of the critical points. You need to plan both these and the arguments you intend to put forward to support your position. If you present a compelling argument, this will lead to your achieving your planned Outcome.

Applying this formula is not just for the big picture in terms of 'what is the outcome I'm looking for in resolving this dispute?' The formula applies to each problem situation. In order to resolve it, you need to know your desired outcome and then decide on the strategy and approach to achieve it.

The success of each meeting builds on the next, and after a series of meetings with successful outcomes, you should have a successful overall resolution to your escalation or dispute.

As you walk into each meeting, you and your team need a clear agenda as to what to raise, how you plan to discuss the topics, and the outcome you seek from that meeting alone. If you do this on a repeat basis for every meeting related to the situation then then you will stay focused and have a much greater chance of success in achieving your big picture outcome.

There is no 'one' approach

There is no single approach that works every time. Each situation must be assessed in its own right with its own set of circumstances. Each situation is affected by the relationship between your company and your client and the people in both organisations.

Culture is a significant factor in the different ways to handle the same situation. Culture in regard to your client's organisation, the country in which you are doing business, the background of the people you are dealing with within that organisation, and those within the project and that specific situation. And then of course there is the personality of the individuals themselves, their values, personal culture and the way in which they do business, which all come under the umbrella of culture.

I have worked across Asia-Pacific and in Europe so cultural diversity has been a significant factor in determining my approach. For example, in Asia-Pacific there are differences in the culture of each Asian country, how they respect people, how they talk to people, and how you need to respect and talk to them.

Different cultural standards and behaviours make a huge difference to how to resolve an escalation. Just because one approach worked last time in a particular country or industry doesn't mean it will work again with a different company or client.

Key behaviours and cultural styles to consider include:

- Are they passive and patient?
- Are they loud and aggressive?
- Are they reasonable?
- Are they dictatorial?
- Are they respectful?
- Are they confrontational?

- Are they litigious?
- What is the structure of their workplace? Is it hierarchical or more decentralised?
- Are there external influences, seen or unseen, that should be considered?

And when you need to use interpreters to communicate, you add yet another layer of complexity to the situation.

Understanding the cultural nuances of the country, the company and the people you are dealing with plays an extremely important part in determining the approach you should take and how you communicate both verbally and in writing.

Who's who in the zoo

Before you first walk into a meeting room or boardroom, there are a number of key considerations you need to plan for prior to the meeting. One major consideration includes assessing your audience, including the level of seniority you will be engaging with on the client side. For example, is the client represented by a person who is a more senior level of management than you have on your team, or are you negotiating with people on an equal level?

This is important, because a more senior figure is likely to put demands on the table that their juniors wouldn't, and most likely push harder to get their way.

If possible, I would recommend that you try and find out who will be attending the meeting. You can look at the attendee list on the calendar invitation and see who has confirmed, but you should always be ready for a surprise when someone unexpected walks in.

The audience is a very important factor. Will only the people who work or have worked on the project be at the meeting? Or has the situation been escalated and a senior or executive figure will be there?

When you are seated, you should look around the table and quickly assess the different personality types in the room. Has the client brought in people who like to take control and be the loudest voice in the room, or have they brought in someone who is quiet, but knows everything that happened and will put forward strong arguments?

You may find that there is a decision-maker or key person of influence in the room who remains quiet and says very little until a decision or a demand needs to be made.

It's very important to help you decide on the approach that you are going to take that you assess all of these factors.

Preparing for the meeting

It is vitally important that in your preparation for a meeting, you look at which issues your client will bring up. For each of those issues you must have a suitably qualified person to help you to manage the topic or address any arguments.

It is possible that your client will set the agenda for the meeting, and if they do it can work to your advantage as it will show what they see as important, which gives you an insight into their priorities.

Even when we identify a number of issues or concerns at the centre of a complaint or escalation, we may be unsure of the highest priority. What we think is important is not always what the client considers the most important, so when they set the agenda it helps you to focus on what answers they want, and you can turn this to your advantage.

If your client doesn't propose an agenda, then it gives you the opportunity to show leadership and manage the relationship, to set the agenda and use it as a precedent for future meetings. You can decide what you want to discuss and make sure you have people present to provide answers on those subjects.

For example, when I go into a meeting if project management is an issue I want discussed, I will make sure the project manager is there because they have all the details of the delivery schedule and issues; if I want to discuss technical issues, I have a technical person present who can address decisions that have been made on a technical level.

Ideally, I have no more than four people on my team at a meeting – three plus myself – but I always have a minimum of two, myself and at least one other as an Insurance policy in the form of a witness. They are there so that no one can accuse me of having promised or having said something untrue.

They can also take notes on what is discussed to avoid anything being misunderstood and thrown at you at a later date.

A question I am often asked, and in fact one that I always consider for myself for each dispute is whether to have a lawyer in the room.

It is important to remember that your role in a dispute or escalation is to try and stop it from going legal. Your role is to find out what went wrong and what is needed to fix the situation. So it stands to reason you will not suggest involving a lawyer.

When I meet with a client, I explain that I am there to stop this from going legal, and I confirm that neither party wants to go down the legal route. This is usually met with a resounding…'let's avoid anything legal.'

However, there are times when a client has their own agenda, and decides before we have even discussed it that they are going to bring their lawyers to the meeting. When confronted with this situation, I ask "Why do we need to have a lawyer in the room?" Their response is often "Oh don't worry about them, our management makes us include our legal people, but the reality is they are just going to listen and make some notes."

Well, don't believe it!

If your client informs you there will be a lawyer in the room, you must immediately talk to your own legal team.

These are the scenarios that may play out:

1. You ask your lawyer to attend because the client's lawyer will be present

2. You ask the client if their lawyer's presence is necessary, and if they insist, you say your lawyer will also attend, and arrange the meeting accordingly

3. You ask your client whether having a lawyer is what both parties want, given your company's intent to resolve matters amicably. The client may realise they are being aggressive and should let the negotiations play out before including their lawyer again.

Having lawyers at a meeting is a serious action because they are not really there to tick the box and check that things are going well. They are there to take detailed notes and step in to correct any misunderstandings on legal and contractual obligations.

Most importantly, they will note everything relevant that was said and by whom, holding you to your word at a later date should they need to.

There are ways around this, such as both parties asking and agreeing upfront for the meeting to proceed 'Without Prejudice'. This means what is said in the meeting as a genuine attempt to resolve a dispute is off the record. It cannot be repeated outside the meeting or used in court as evidence of admissions against the party that made them.

It is best to ask your legal team about these situations and how to handle the request for a lawyer to be in attendance. You need sound advice, and every situation is different – this really is on a case-by-case basis.

Earlier I wrote that I suggest you have no more than four people at a meeting. This is because sometimes that can be quite intimidating for the client, or there just end up being too many people in the room, especially if the client has the same number attending.

It is very important that you make sure that you are represented by people of equal management level so that there is no seniority power play or intimidation. If your client's CIO is attending the meeting, that can make a powerful difference in terms of decision-making and also their ability to influence a discussion. You need to be respectful and can't necessarily challenge them as you would like to, but that could put you at a disadvantage in the negotiation.

In such a case, you should consider bringing in someone from your organisation of equal standing in the corporate hierarchy, not necessarily your CIO, but perhaps a general manager, or delivery or account executive. You will still run the meeting but have them to call upon if and when you need.

In preparing for any meeting, you should try to find out in advance how many people will be there and who will represent the client. Do your homework on each person's job title and, if possible, their personality and style. Are they aggressive or soft? Loud or quiet? Hot-headed, or cool and calm? A talker or a thinker? Technical or strategic?

Find out where they sit in the hierarchy of the project? Are they a contractor or employee, and if the latter, how long have they been with the company?

You can find out these details from people who have worked on the project or who manage the client's account in your company. It is likely that people in your company will have worked with some or all of those attending on the client's side.

You should do your homework and understand as much about them as you can - their personalities, roles and relationships prior to the meeting. Based on this information, you choose your team and discuss how you will interact with each other as part of your approach.

Just as you need to assess the audience in terms of who will be representing the client at the meeting, you must also make the same assessment of your team. Who should represent you? All these factors come in to play and form the approach that you take in order to get the best outcome.

Whom do you need on your team?

In the escalation or dispute process, once you have the findings from your investigation, you are ready to meet with the client to discuss the contentious issues that have been raised. This is the start of the resolution process, and while there is a long way to go, no matter how many meetings are needed, you need to plan well for each. To resolve an escalation or dispute always requires a series of meetings where you work through each of the issues and provide answers.

For each of these meetings you should apply the S+A = O formula and decide whom to take along to the meetings

Avoid where possible going into a meeting alone, as the only person representing your company, especially if there are several people representing the client. You want to go in with a team, whose members will each play a role, and be confident from the outset that you have the right people there to support you in achieving the outcome you have planned for.

The people you take to the meeting should be based on the knowledge, skills or expertise they bring to the table as well as having the right type of personality. You need to be confident that they will help you achieve the desired result.

The significance of the makeup of the team is often overlooked, but it's a crucial tactic that can make all the difference between success or failure.

When putting together your team, you need to take into account all of the factors that I have previously mentioned. That includes knowing who will be attending on behalf of the client, their status, background and culture, and their level of knowledge of the project. These are all factors that you need to take into account in your planning sessions and when determining the team that you want to bring along with you.

Overall the team needs to align with the agreed strategy you plan to lead with in the meeting.

You have to be sure your team will follow your lead, so don't bring anyone who likes to be the loudest voice in the room, since they are likely to derail your strategy and that can turn any meeting into an absolute disaster - which I have seen happen.

In fact, it happened to me on one escalation when someone's ego got in the way and they decided to take matters into their own hands. They made ridiculous promises they could never keep, and while the client was impressed at the time, it hurt our chances of success when they failed to deliver only weeks later.

While you can't always control every individual, at the end of the day you are all representing your company, and the client is only interested in how your company is going about resolving their complaint. An egocentric person in your team who goes off script, making promises they can't keep, makes no difference to the client. Promises are promises and the disappointment when they are not kept will be damaging.

Having the wrong person on the team and in the room ends up taking more effort to manage and takes away your focus on resolving the situation.

The team you select must be able to work with and support you, so you can focus your time and energy on what will be discussed.

The importance of being face-to-face

Nowadays with advanced technology and a greater-than-ever reliance on emails and communication platforms, people have forgotten the value of being face-to-face. This is even more the case when dealing with escalations and disputes.

Of course the challenges of a global pandemic have made face-to-face meetings impossible, but when businesses find new protocols around travel and physical meetings are back again, it will highlight the value of meeting with your clients, sitting in their office and working through their issues.

There is so much to gain from meeting clients face-to-face, and they value it even more when someone goes to that amount of effort to deal with a problem.

I have been known to travel from Australia to parts of Asia that could take anywhere up to 15 hours, just to attend a two-hour meeting with the client because I judged it was important to meet them face-to-face. It shows your client a genuine commitment to make an effort to engage with them.

Face-to-face meetings show a clear intention to take pro-active responsibility for the situation, a true willingness to talk openly and commitment to a resolution. There's a lot of research around the percentage conveyed by non-verbal and verbal communication, but most settles around 30% for the words you use and 70% for the non-verbal signs you give: tone of voice, how you sit, facial expression, how much you listen, and how much eye contact you make.

Separate but connected is understanding your own communication style. On the emotional side, how empathetic are you? Are you a hard or soft person to talk to? Do you build rapport easily with your client?

Understanding your own emotional intelligence enables you to choose your words when you acknowledge the pain a client shares with you in that first meeting. It also enables you to be very clear about your role in the process for resolving the issue.

A one-to-one meeting enables you to make eye contact which should not be underestimated when it comes to showing your level of care. It is extremely difficult to build rapport on this level over the phone, in an email or even on Teams/Zoom. Only 7% of our messages in a conversation are conveyed by words, so no wonder email isn't the best way to resolve an issue.

Face-to-face takes away the guesswork for the client about whom they are working with and relying on to help address their pain and allows you to find out first-hand whom you are dealing with. It also gives you the opportunity to show quite quickly that you are sympathetic to the client's issues and perspective and to understand why they are upset about the situation.

Another significant benefit of face-to-face meetings is that, initially, the meeting is not about providing solutions or answers: it's about listening to them, and from these initial meetings you build a level of trust and rapport.

For every face-to-face meeting, you need a clear set of objectives, especially in a situation like mine, when you consider how far I may have travelled for a relatively short meeting. A clear agenda and objectives ensure that the meeting gives me the best value.

The priorities for meetings to resolve an issue are really clear:

1. Establish the relationship
2. Get the facts

These two core components will carry you through. Your initial face-to-face meetings, your intention should be to manage the situation via email and phone conversations as you work through to a resolution. You should not set a precedent where you need to travel back and forth in order to get results.

My objectives for all initial face-to-face meetings are to make sure that:

1. The client gains the confidence that they can work with me and together we can achieve a resolution

2. I establish credibility and show that I can actually make a difference and be relevant in my ability to influence the situation.

Based on my experience, these objectives would not be possible if they didn't meet with me face-to-face, especially when they are already in complaint mode and quick to criticise your company.

It is a lot easier to yell at someone over the phone than it is face-to-face. When the client can look you in the eye and really talk to you, and when you can show you are there to listen, it makes it harder for them to be aggressive and angry.

In these situations, the client will respect you for being prepared to meet and take ownership of resolving the issue. Again these are the credibility, trust and confidence elements that will work for you.

In most of these meetings I also explain to the client that I am the client advocate, and I am there to be their voice within my organisation. Therefore, I can take back a message to my executive management and board. This gives them access and a voice within our organisation, and when they realise that it almost always changes the dynamic in the relationship.

I let them know that I am authorised to represent the company and that we are committed to resolving the issue, so if they explain their issues to me, I will communicate them and the reasons behind their position to my organisation. Most clients know that having their voice heard inside a large organisation is usually extremely difficult.

Leave your ego at the door

The world-renowned music producer Quincy Jones tells the story: "At the famed recording of We Are The World for USA for Africa on 28 January 1985, as the room filled with a mind-boggling array of talent, each artist was famously greeted with a sign that instructed them to 'check your egos at the door'.

That is more of a fun fact than anything else, but it does have some relevance to managing an escalation.

When it comes to fronting up to any meeting involving the management of a commercial escalation or dispute, it is very important that you and your team don't bring your egos into a meeting.

Irrespective of whether you think the client is right or wrong, whether you feel that they have overreacted, or escalated a situation when it was not warranted, if you bring that perspective into the meeting, it is your ego talking, and clients will always see and feel it.

The client will sense that you don't really value what they have said and have not come to the meeting prepared to listen. They will believe that you are not there to resolve matters fairly but have already made up your mind. These are the problems that egos bring to such situations.

People who like to be the loudest voice in the room believe they have all the answers and like to do things their way are the ones you need to be careful of. These behaviours and personality types pose the biggest challenge in terms of keeping them under control.

From my experience, when you put together your team for an escalation, be wary of big egos. They will likely derail your efforts and will not follow your lead. You spend more time worrying about them and what they could possibly say in a meeting that may upset any progress you are making.

The last thing you need in your meeting is to have someone who suggests that they know better or think they are better. There is no place for ego, and no need for it either. Egos only get in the way.

Escalation meetings need people who are calm, compassionate, empathetic and prepared to listen. You must have emotional intelligence and be committed to looking after the client and the relationship, and be focused on achieving a fair and reasonable outcome.

A key element to this is knowing that you are not the smartest person in the room, and you don't need to be the loudest either.

You can't go into any meeting assuming that everything 'we' did was right. Your ego will get in the way if you think that you are right and you are simply arguing your position.

It is important that you go into meetings with a very clear objective, and your approach will help determine that. Work out in advance what you want to get out of this meeting, the outcome you are looking for. It's a win if you can walk out and tick the box that you got what you wanted, no matter how small the step. Every step and every positive meeting takes you one step further to rebuilding the relationship with your client.

How to keep your emotions out of the room

The facts are the anchor for you to hold on to when dealing with egos and emotions. They provide the support you need to manage emotion in a meeting. The facts are your lifeline, which is why I am so insistent on the importance of following the comprehensive process to gather the facts by keeping detailed written records so that you have the evidence to stand up to any challenges a client may present.

It becomes much easier to refute challenges from a client when you can clearly articulate what happened,

"This is what our findings have discovered, through a series of interviews that have been conducted; this is what I can confirm happened based on documented evidence that supports these facts."

This is a strong position that few could argue, especially when they haven't done any of the investigation that you have carried out to support your position. A fact-based approach will outsmart a point of view based purely on emotion every time.

When you do this and present yourself in a down-to-earth, grounded way, with a fact-based approach that can be supported by documented evidence, it is easy to keep emotions out of the environment and out of the room.

It doesn't matter how the client reacts: they may be angry or upset, and they may insist on factors that they believe happened, but if those don't align with the facts uncovered in the investigation it becomes very easy to stand by your findings.

Situations usually become heated when two people get emotional. Therefore, if only one person is emotional and the other remains calm and keeps their emotions out of the discussion, the situation can be defused very quickly.

The facts allow you to keep emotion out of it. The process you have followed ensures they have been established before you go into a meeting, and prepares you for the meetings and negotiations to follow.

I am often asked how I deal with angry clients and stop situations from stressing me and getting to me emotionally. The answer is that it is mostly through your mindset and ability to prepare mentally for a difficult conversation.

When you know you are walking into a difficult meeting, there is no element of surprise. In other words, when you go in expecting something to happen and it happens, then you are much more prepared for it than if you didn't see it coming. In preparing for a meeting, I always ask myself how bad can this get? In the scheme of things, especially when you have an idea of what may be coming, it is not that bad most of the time.

When you are going to see an angry client, who has sent a letter of complaint or escalation, then you know that the meeting will be heated and emotional. So you are ready for it. You always hope that it will not be as bad as that and when it does happen it is a pleasant surprise and a bonus – but you can't count on that.

In preparing yourself emotionally, remember you are there to represent your company. You are the company ambassador. Your client is having a go at your company, and you are simply representing it.

You didn't cause the problem, but you are there to help fix it. Having this mindset and approach means that you do not go into a meeting feeling defensive. You do not feel a need to apologise, because you personally have not done anything wrong. You have been sent in to try and resolve the situation. Don't lose sight of this as a positive and not a negative.

The criticisms and anger that you might feel from across the table are almost never directed at you personally – remember it can't be personal when they have never met you before.

My approach is to make sure they understand my role and how I plan to go about helping them. It is important they understand that I'm not part of the problem but part of the solution, however that initial meeting or phone call is not the time to try and make them understand. Usually their emotion stops them from hearing anything positive, so you need to wait until it's the right time, which is usually once they have vented and dealt with their anger, disappointment or frustration. This is the reason why it is important to encourage them to get things off their chest and put all issues on the table. Only then will they be ready to listen and understand your role.

It is important that you explain that you are not like anyone who has previously tried to resolve the situation. Whatever you promise you must be accountable for. You should not make any promises that you can't keep, or you will be seen just like the others who failed, at least in the client's eyes.

Accountability goes hand in hand with credibility, so never make promises you can't keep. Take the hit for what has gone wrong and manage their emotions, then move the conversation forward once they have got it all out of their systems.

How to deal with personal attacks

Escalations are not usually personal, unless you were part of the project team and didn't perform so the client doesn't think that highly of you. Then the comments may refer directly to you, but otherwise comments and criticisms are not usually directed at anyone on a personal level.

However, you should know how to deal with situations that do become personal. Heightened emotions can sometimes, unnecessarily, turn into something more personal. Your client may turn on you personally, as in their eyes you represent the company and you're the person sitting across the table from them.

Of course there is no situation where anyone has the right to be abusive or attack you or anyone in your team personally. If you find yourself in a situation that has become personal, then you have every right to make it very clear that you feel uncomfortable with the way you are being spoken to and ask that this stops immediately.

You should also make it clear that if it happens again you will call an end to the meeting or phone call and resume when the person has regained their composure.

If it does happen again, then you must follow through with your threat and end the meeting politely, diplomatically and professionally. You need to decide whether you are prepared to meet with them again, or continue to engage with them via email only. You may even decide to request the abuser be removed and someone else assigned as your point of contact.

You don't have to be in a position of authority to make this decision. The nature of a personal abuse situation gives everyone the right and authority to do what is necessary.

I would also recommend you send an email to your organisation and discuss with someone internally how this should be best communicated to the client - whether direct to the abuser and cc their manager, or only to their manager. You may also want to ask someone more senior in your organisation whom you already know and trust, to seek their advice on how this should be communicated to the client.

When I discuss this topic, people say they often feel powerless because of the status or seniority of the abuser, for example if it is a senior executive. A person's position in an organisation does not exempt them from decent behaviour. Irrespective of title or level of seniority, every person has the right to be respected in any professional situation.

That said, it is important to distinguish between an attack of a personal nature and a client's comments and criticisms of the company. In general, when it comes to commercial complaints it is rarely personal. As you are the company's representative, when the client is criticising you or the team's performance, poor delivery or supposed misrepresentation during the sales process, they are complaining about the company and not you personally. After all you are there to manage the complaint.

Although what is being said is being directed at you, you should not mistake it as being about you. You need to see criticism for what it is and listen with the right mindset, so that you don't take it personally.

Nonetheless, make notes, acknowledge the complaint being made and, in your role, address their pain points and work with them to resolve the problem.

 TIP

Steps to deal with a personal attack

1. Make it very clear that you are uncomfortable with the way you are being spoken to and ask that it stop immediately.

2. If it happens again, call an end to the meeting and make it clear that you will resume at another time when the person has regained their composure.

3. Send an email to your organisation documenting the incident and discuss internally with someone senior how this should best be communicated to the client.

4. Inform the client in writing.

The order to raise issues

In the fact-gathering process (page 26, The First Meeting) I wrote about the importance of taking notes and this is where your detailed notes come into play and will be most beneficial.

As you plan your client meeting, you need to put together the agenda of items for discussion. Your client will be expecting answers and will want to know what you have done in response to the issues raised at the first meeting.

The order in which you raise these issues for discussion will have a direct effect on the success of the meeting.

Part of your approach and strategy towards resolution should be to take advantage of quick wins wherever possible to create a positive tone in any negotiation forum.

When preparing the meeting agenda, look through the pain points in your notes and see which have been resolved through actions already taken, and the items where your company has accepted responsibility for what went wrong.

These are the 'quick wins' and should come first on the agenda so that from the start of your meeting as these issues are discussed, it creates a positive energy and mood.

Where the client may have thought that every item on that list was going to be a challenge, which would create an 'us versus them' environment, they will see straight away that your company has accepted responsibility or taken positive action to fix certain things that were in dispute or wrong.

This allows you to push back on other items for which your company has not accepted responsibility, or where the actions to resolve other issues have not been as immediate or decisive.

The client will feel more positive if the meeting is opened in this way, and the quick wins for them will make them feel that they have made good progress, so that any pushback on the other items as the discussion unfolds should not be as harsh as it might otherwise have been.

This more positive mood will be the direct result of the items you choose to raise first.

Lose the fear of upsetting the client

People have a real fear of telling the client something they don't want to hear at the risk of ruining the relationship and the impact that may have on future opportunities. The fact of the matter is that you need to lose that fear.

There is one word that people find the most difficult to say to a client and that word is 'no'.

For example,
Is the project still running on time?
Does your team have the solution to this problem?
Is your company going to pay for this change in scope?
The answer to questions and scenarios like these should be 'no' but due to the fear of upsetting a client, people find it hard to say no. Unfortunately, the consequences of not saying no when you should, can be disastrous. They are escalations waiting to happen.

When you know the project is no longer running on time and has been hit by a new issue, by not telling the truth you are setting the wrong expectation with the client. They were concerned that the project might have fallen behind schedule, however you are assuring them that it is still running on time, although you know you can no longer meet the original timeline.

When a new problem or challenge arises, all too often people are fearful of admitting that they don't have the answers yet, although not necessarily because it is their fault. There is nothing wrong with admitting it, as long as you have a plan and a timeline to give them.

When there's any change to the scope, companies are usually most concerned about who's going to pay. When no is the correct answer commercially and contractually, you have to be upfront and tell them the truth.

Another situation is when you have to tell the client something they don't want to hear:

For example, if we discover during the fact-gathering something that the client has done wrong or is responsible for that they are not aware of:

"After investigating the issue further, we have discovered that your team failed to do what they were responsible for. Unfortunately, this caused the problem and the delays that we have today."

OR

"We looked into this problem and found that, as per the contract, it was your team's responsibility to do that task, and not our team's responsibility."

You need to learn that telling the truth and saying it as it is, is okay.

As hard as it is to do so, the consequences are much worse if you don't. It takes practice to handle objections and have tough conversations, and the fear of upsetting the client should not prevent you from saying what needs to be said.

My advice on how to best confront these conversations is:

1. **Never personalise the message.**
   Always keep it about the company or the organisation by avoiding the word 'you'. The word 'you' makes it personal - about them specifically. Then they feel under attack and go into denial and self-defence mode.

   Avoid making statements such as 'I think you did this wrong' or 'it would appear that you did this....'

   You can soften that message by saying:

   'This is what we understand happened...

   After checking the contract, it would appear that this is one of your company's action items and was not completed.'

   If it's based on fact and you know it's the truth, then you have to tell the client exactly what they need to know. That means you must lose the fear of upsetting them.

   You must always be diplomatic and professional, but still tell the client what they don't want to hear. After all, this is business and you are there to get a job done.

2. **Basing it on the facts makes it much easier to say no.**
   The facts are the foundation you are basing your position on – they represent what happened in the past and they are what you must rely upon for making decisions today. If the facts support your position, then being upfront and truthful should not be a concern.

For both of these situations, how you deliver the message matters most.

Beware of personal agendas

Sometimes when dealing with an escalation, no matter how hard you study the facts and examine the situation, a client takes a particular position and won't let it go. Such situations make you question what they are thinking.

I have experienced this a few times, when a client puts forward an argument that they can't support. It is often not the first thing that I will think of until a few comments or accusations don't add up, that I realise that someone is pushing a personal agenda and wishing for a particular outcome irrespective of the facts.

Tactics include making up facts or throwing in comments to make you doubt someone's version of what happened, perhaps to steer you in the wrong direction. These people are knowingly throwing a grenade over the fence and waiting for it to blow up!

Personal agendas are calculated and almost always driven by self-interest. The person is looking for an outcome that benefits them. It may make them look good with their superiors, it may be detrimental to a colleague they are in competition with. They may have promised their direct report to improve their profile within the company. There are any number of possible reasons, so when they sense that the door is slightly ajar in a meeting, it's an opportunity for them to seize what they want.

The important point is don't forget or ignore that personal agendas exist. When you are investigating a situation and someone's view doesn't align with the other facts, then ask yourself is there a personal agenda that I need to consider?

I prefer to think of other people as reasonable, however a personal agenda usually explains everything going on. Once you know what's happening it is much easier to work out how to move forward towards resolving the situation.

Let's summarise

1. Make the effort to arrange a face-to-face meeting with your client

2. Remember your objectives are to:
   - Establish a relationship to build confidence, trust and credibility
   - Gather the facts. Be clear what you want to achieve from the meeting

3. Explain your role as the client advocate and how you can help get them to be heard, but without making any promises about the outcome

4. Let them know how you plan to manage the process including the ongoing communication, by email and telephone.

The Negotiation

The Negotiation is the final aspect of the escalation process

We have established a relationship with our client and set some boundaries around how we will deal with the escalation or dispute. We have investigated and determined the facts and we have decided on our approach. We have put together a strategy that includes deciding on our team and we are clear on our position on each of the items in discussion.

We are now ready to meet with the client and negotiate to resolve the issues.

When we discussed the approach, I explained the importance of breaking down the process into a series of bite-size negotiations where you determine the Strategy, Approach and Outcome for every meeting. Every meeting is a negotiation, and each successful outcome is an achievement and a step closer to the big picture outcome – which is resolving the escalation or dispute.

We will now explore ways in which you can achieve the outcome you're looking for.

Asking for too much

We often don't know where to start when it comes to negotiating a position and outcome, especially the financial outcome of a dispute situation.

At the beginning of our engagement in the escalation, we ask the client what it is they are looking for – action or money or both?

Whatever the response, it needs to be factored into our negotiation. What are we prepared to do and what are we not prepared to do?

Going into a meeting with a planned outcome is very similar to going to an auction. You know what you would like to pay and the maximum amount that you're prepared to bid up to. This way when you get caught up in the emotion of the auction, as you do, if your number is clear in your mind then when the bidding reaches that or goes above, the decision is simple and you're out.

There are many ways in which to strategise a negotiation. If you make a clear decision for yourself about where you want the negotiation to end up, then whatever twists, turns and mind games you have to play along the way become irrelevant. Where you end up is all that matters - how you got there doesn't.

Often in an escalation, your client will make a seemingly ridiculous request. If they feel they have been wronged, they may seek an excessive amount of compensation – an ambit claim.

You have to start a negotiation from your most comfortable position and leave enough room to achieve your preferred outcome. When you know that your client's position is too far away from yours, you make your position clear, and this will set the tone for the negotiation.

When it comes to compensation claims most companies refuse to make straight 'cash' payments. However a client is often not interested in listening to what they don't want to hear and may continue to repeat their demands despite the fact that you have already indicated a payout is not an option.

So what do you do?

My approach is to make my position clear from the start the meeting. This can sometimes be seen as a bold statement, but it's something that needs to be established.

I open the meeting by explaining that while I understand the client is continuing to ask for a payout, that is not our company policy as I have explained before, so we will not be open to any compensation that includes a payout.

You should be prepared for this strategy to inflame the situation, but this is one way to set the tone.

In reality, there may be a small sum of money you can negotiate with, or you may be able to offer some form of service in lieu of a payout but taking such a strong stance upfront resets expectation. Since you have made such a blunt statement the client realises that they have to reduce their demands substantially if they are to come anywhere close to your zero position, as opposed to thinking that they may be able to win you over.

 **TIP**

Shifting the conversation and the negotiation

Let's use the example of buying a car:

The dealer quotes the list price of $68,000, but indicates that they are prepared to sell it to you for $60,000. You are prepared to pay $52,000. The dealer has already told you that $60,000 is absolutely their lowest price – how often have you heard them say – "at this price there is no profit in it for us". But we know that's never true.

In this situation I would tell the dealer that I have $45,000 to spend, and therefore $60,000 is way out of my range. I may also say that I might be able to scrape together a little bit more money but right now I am at $45,000. After a lot of posturing I indicate that $50,000 may be possible for me if I borrow some money from family, so that is only assuming I can get those funds.

I expect the dealer's reaction to my offer of $45,000 to be that my price is way too low and there's no way the car can be sold at that price. From my point of view though I've taken the negotiation away from $60,000 or thereabouts and repositioned it at a far lower price – definitely a lot closer to $50,000. And because I'm only talking high 40s/low 50s, any higher sum has been taken off the table.

From a strategic perspective, they are no longer going to try and transact the business at $60,000 because I'm at $45,000 trying to get to $50,000. They are at $60,000 and they need to come down significantly to get close to my $50,000.

So if I'm prepared to pay $52,000 for the car, starting at $45,000 and compromising on $52,000 is a lot easier and a lot less emotional than bargaining from $68,000 down to $60,000 and then trying to work out how to get to $52,000.

Can you see how the conversation and negotiation have shifted?

My advice is to set the tone of the negotiation so that you can control where it starts and, hopefully, where it ends. Have a clear price in mind and don't get emotionally dragged into the negotiation.

Ways to influence a negotiation stalemate

It is important to remember that in a negotiation, only a 'fair and reasonable' outcome for both parties is what is needed to settle a dispute. In mediation circles, you know you have achieved this when both parties are not particularly happy with the settlement. One party considers that they gave away a little more than they would have liked, and the other party feels that they wanted a little bit more but accepted what they settled on for the sake of agreement and moving forward.

However very often a situation becomes a stalemate, and your negotiation appears to be going nowhere. Here are a few strategies or tactics that may help create a shift in the stalemate and some tips to regain control of a meeting:

The loudest voice in the room

In a meeting consider who is dominating the room on the client's side. It may be that the person with the loudest voice is doing all the talking and not working with you to try and achieve a mutual outcome - they're working for their own outcome. Or you may notice that the same few people around the table are dominating the discussion. Either situation often leads to a stalemate.

To break the stalemate:

1. Ask the people at the table who haven't said much, especially those on the client's team whom you feel may be cooperative, what they think about the topic under discussion.

   Very often the individuals around the table may not be in agreement or aligned with the leader, but the leader is doing all the talking and no one dares to interrupt. You can force a change by turning to the person you want to speak up and saying to them;

   "John, I'm very keen to hear your thoughts on this topic?"

   or

   "I'd like to ask John if he would share his thoughts and perspective on this topic as I would really value his opinion."

   The fact that you are showing respect and value for someone on the other team can sometimes work in your favour especially for that person, who will now feel obliged to give their view. Even if you don't really know John's view and it could work against you, it is still the approach to take to get someone else speaking and to change the dynamic.

   Getting someone else to speak creates the opportunity for others to enter the discussion and play to your advantage, especially if they're not even on your team.

2. Bring in a senior figure such as a well-respected executive from your company, or someone whom you know the client will listen to. This relates to the topic we previously discussed about the importance of the people in your team. Directly or indirectly, this can influence the rest of the room, because everyone knows this person is a key decision-maker.

I want to reinforce the point that these decisions are strategic and none of this happens without planning. Make this part of your strategy that you have agreed prior to the meeting and explain to your team how and when you will use it. Again, it highlights the importance of strategising your approach.

In a stalemate situation, what you're trying to do is disrupt the flow of the meeting and exert some control. Asking someone new to speak may change the dynamic of the discussion, and it also takes control from the other party because you are dictating who should be speaking.

Strategically you have picked John specifically because you're hoping he will say something that works in your favour, however there is a risk that he doesn't agree and you don't have the ally you hoped for and may need to rethink your position and the arguments.

But bringing other people into the discussion can enable a shift, especially where the client has taken an unreasonable position.

Obviously, calling on the opinions of members of your team may also be able to change the tone of the meeting.

Call for a break

Another tactic in a stalemate is to call a break to the negotiation even if it's just for 10 minutes. You can say "Let's take 10 minutes for a coffee" or even "I would like a short 10 minutes to meet with my team if that's okay."

You may do this for a number of reasons:

1. If your team or the client's team appear to be frazzled, tired or losing focus then this is the opportunity to regroup. For your own team, you may decide to do it to realign, make sure that you are sticking to the plan or to discuss points

that have been raised which may have some legitimacy. You may genuinely need to discuss what is going on before you continue down the path that you are on.

It is extremely important in any negotiation that you continually assess and re-assess your position, because in a dynamic environment when certain factors are raised it may be reasonable to consider them seriously, especially a legal point that may have some validity.

2. You may feel that you have argued a strong point and your client is still not listening; or you may find someone on your team has spoken out and not stuck to the plan. They may say things that were not in the script and which have steered the conversation down the wrong path. All valid reasons to call for a break.
3. Equally, the client team may have an agitator interfering with the flow of the meeting and derailing the conversation from your perspective when you had thought it was on the right path.

I liken the idea of a break to injury time in a tennis match. Sometimes a player will take a convenient 10-minute 'injury' break because they want to change the flow of the match. They feel they are being dominated and know that interrupting the concentration of the other player with a break will put things on an even footing again, perhaps changing the fortunes of the game.

My approach is that if I call for a break, it is so that the teams can re-align and re-assess their position. Most of the time, people don't think to call for a break; they forget and tend to continue to push through.

These tips are not limited to commercial discussions or matters in dispute with a financial outcome. You can use these tactics whenever there is healthy debate. For example, agreeing on change requests, priority lists, scoping requirements or general disagreements - all common challenges during the implementation of a project.

A good escalation manager will always monitor the progress of discussions from both sides of the table – and focus on making decisions that you can see benefits from.

Let's summarise

In a stalemate where you are not making any progress:

1. Open up the discussion to include other people at the table who haven't said much and ask their opinion.

2. Decide when it is the right time for the senior figure at the table to speak.

3. Call for a break when you feel either team needs to regroup or realign, or just to reconsider your position and strategy. Obviously, this depends on how the negotiation is going and what you stand to gain from the break.

The lifecycle of commercial disputes and escalations

To recap:

None of these concepts and ideas stands alone - they are intertwined, integrated and interdependent to achieve the ultimate success, which is avoiding commercial escalations and, where you can't avoid them, managing them to an acceptable and satisfactory outcome.

If you adopt best practices, then you raise the standards of project delivery and reduce the number of commercial escalations, and escalations overall. You do this by making sure that you:

Document better - conversations, decisions and all agreed actions

Communicate better - keeping stakeholders and executive sponsors better informed on a regular basis and by providing answers to their questions in advance. Keeping project teams aligned, so there is less chance of disjointed project delivery. Understanding your audience and crafting emails to suit them, always communicating in good time so that everyone who needs to know is informed.

Stay **Accountable** by keeping your promises, setting deadlines, and managing expectations so that nobody feels disappointed or is left wondering what is happening.

If you do all these things better, then you reduce the number of problems that we know lead to disputes, escalations and unhappy clients. In the event that you find yourself in escalation, then focus on three key things – Relationship, Approach and Outcome.

Look after the client **Relationship** by making sure that they are listened to and inform them of the process that you will follow: to investigate issues that have been raised using a fact-based approach to determine your position. We do this to ensure that we are making decisions that are not based on people's opinions, perceptions or interpretations of what happened, but based on the facts of what actually happened.

Adopt an **Approach** to resolve an issue following the formula where you first determine what the outcome is you want to achieve in the overall situation, and then break it down into smaller parts.

Apply the same formula, whether it's for one meeting or a series of meetings, and make sure that before each meeting you decide on the **Outcome** you wish to achieve, then the strategy that you will adopt and the approach to best achieve your outcome. Problem by problem, meeting by meeting, escalation by escalation.

About Ashley

For as long as I can remember, whenever there was a problem, I would put my hand up to fix it.

I have always had a knack for sorting out problems and I am rarely daunted by the problem itself. In fact, I thrive on the challenge.

I have always thought that my mind is like a filing cabinet – there are lots of drawers, folders, dividers and tabs, and everything is in some kind of order. When it comes to solving problems, I can visualise what the outcome should look like and my logical thought process figures it out step by step. My approach is to eliminate the factors that are irrelevant one at a time, until I find what has really caused the problem. By doing this I work out where the problem really stems from.

How did I find out that I had this problem-solving skill? Well, it's instinct, although I thought everyone had the ability to solve problems in the same that way that I do. For many years I didn't think it was anything special, and to some extent even today I still think most people know what I know.

In my career, for more than 30 years I have been a fixer. I have fixed problems in technology – in the early days of networks, software and hardware – and I have fixed problems in business in areas such as operations, finance and logistics. From computer system crashes, project crises, client disaster situations, disputes and escalations - I've been responsible for fixing them all.

At the beginning of my career, when I started in IT, I worked in a support role for a software company called Solution 6. That was my first taste of technology, and for three years all I did was manage support calls from their clients, which were accounting practices and financial institutions. I also set up network systems and provided training for these businesses, but predominantly my role was solving problems.

In 1989, aged 24, I started my own company, fixing clients' technology problems. My company was their first port of call when anything went wrong with their IT.

It was in these very early days, when I was about 29, that I tasted mediation. I was asked to mediate a dispute between three parties - my client, their hardware provider and the software vendor. The client was implementing a new accounting system along with new hardware. When the software didn't work as it should, the software vendor blamed the hardware company, and the hardware company blamed the software people. All my client knew was they were paying everyone and still didn't have a working solution.

I was engaged as an independent consultant, to help my client work out who was ultimately responsible. I investigated the matter, based on the facts of what actually happened, not what everyone thought happened - it was fact-based, not my opinion. The seed had been sown.

I grew my company, merged with a large accounting firm along the way, and sold my part of the business in 2001.

At the same time, I was approached by Solution 6 again, the company I had worked for 12 years before, and asked back to help them rebuild their Professional Services Division. I found that my role was mainly meeting with clients who had threatened to sue Solution 6 for not delivering new software releases as promised. For two years, I put out fires and stopped the clients from proceeding with legal actions. My 'bomb defusing' skills were becoming very well developed.

In January 2006, I moved to IBM, where I worked in the dispute resolution team looking after major disputes, critical situations and escalations in Australia and New Zealand.

When they offered me the opportunity and explained that I would spend 100% of my time resolving disputes, I had never imagined that such a job existed – and the offer was too good to refuse.

It was the job of a lifetime and it changed my career. Seven years and 517 dispute cases later, I left IBM.

I joined SAP in 2016 and it will come as no surprise that I'm still fixing problems. When I was approached by SAP, it was to trial a new role. They created a job for me to manage their commercial disputes and escalations. The trial started in Australia and New Zealand, and within 12 months was expanded to Asia-Pacific Japan.

Today I am the commercial mediator for SAP, responsible for all commercial disputes and escalations for the company in the Asia-Pacific Japan region.

I am brought in to deal with client disputes and escalations where the client has lodged a formal complaint or a letter of demand, often with a legal threat requesting compensation, damages or something similar. My job is to stop the situation from escalating further and being referred to the lawyers.

I do this by stepping in and taking charge, by establishing a relationship with the client, investigating what really happened and finding a way to resolve the situation that is fair and reasonable to both parties. My job is a mix of mediation, facilitation, people management, negotiation and dispute resolution, and I have enjoyed many great successes.

In parallel, over the past three years I have created and developed the masterclass program *How To Defuse A Bomb* where I share my expertise, advice and insights to help people and organisations to avoid commercial disputes and escalations, or if it is too late to avoid them, to show them how best to manage them and get the best results.

The program is called *How To Defuse A Bomb* in the broader market (outside of SAP) and at SAP it is known as Mastering Commercial Escalations.

I present and facilitate the Mastering Commercial Escalations program at SAP in over 15 countries across Asia-Pacific, Japan and Europe.

My KPI's are my own and they are very simple – resolve every dispute and retain every client. When your core belief is that there is no problem that can't be solved, my KPI's are very achievable.

My job has afforded me to travel the world fixing problems and defusing bombs. This is my dream job.

So, finally, why this book?

Well, after 20+ years in dispute resolution, I've come to realise that I have a lot of knowledge to be shared. My hope is that my insights, advice, tips and experience can help you do a better job avoiding disputes and escalations, or if too late to avoid, then managing them for a better outcome.

About The Program

In the About Ashley section (refer page 104) I wrote about the masterclass program that I created, and which I deliver to SAP and the broader market. This book is a companion to the program content and should be used as a reference guide.

The *How To Defuse a Bomb* masterclass program is designed for those in client-facing roles, both Sales and Services. It is a series of three workshops where I share my experiences, insights, tips and advice on escalation management and the skills needed to have tough conversations and prevent situations turning into escalations.

The program is designed to help participants gain a better understanding of techniques and insights that will build their knowledge and confidence in handling escalations.

The key objectives are;

1. **To improve the skills of the individual**
   – by providing attendees with the tools to better handle themselves in problem and escalated situations; this is done by sharing with tips, techniques and advice on how they can achieve a better outcome to an escalating situation or manage an existing problem scenario

2. **To implement best practice**
   – by providing knowledge and advice to the attendees so that they and the company they work for are better protected in the event of an escalation situation, whether it is a project or engagement.

All the topics in the book are presented in the workshops where I talk in detail on how they can be applied in real dispute and escalation situations.

In each of the three workshops, I follow the same format. There is a Learning session and a Role-Playing session.

Learning Session

This session is a half-day session split into - How To Avoid Escalations and How To Manage Escalations (when too late to avoid).

This is where I talk about topics on the subject of managing problem situations and commercial escalations. The session is interactive, and I encourage the attendees to share their own experiences. This includes discussing situations they have been involved in or are currently dealing with, how they handled the situation, the challenges they faced and how could they have handled it differently to get a better outcome. If it is a current escalation, I use those as examples to give immediate tips, advice and the approach on how best to manage it.

This learning component is topic-based. Depending on the audience, I deliver the full list of topics, or the list can be tailored to suit in which case I present a select group of topics that are specifically relevant to the attendees.

Role Playing Session

The second half-day is a role-playing activity and the objective is for the attendees to put into practice the insights they have gained from the Learning session.

I assign the attendees to play each of the roles of client and vendor. The aim of the exercise is for the participants to apply the learnings from the Learning Session via a test run in a mock client situation.

Throughout each role-play, I coach the attendees and provide real-time advice and guidance to every participant.

The session format utilises the following scenario;

- A vendor (our mock company) has received a complaint letter or a legal letter from the client
- each attendee is placed in group, and they are assigned a case (based on real-life cases)
- each group has to represent the vendor in a mock client meeting to manage the escalation and discuss the letter
- the attendees take on roles as the either the client, or the key person (e.g Account Executive/Relationship Manager/Project Manager/Delivery Lead) who has to manage the client facing meeting with the letter being the subject for discussion
- there is time allocated for preparation and strategic planning prior to the role-playing.

The three workshops represent the lifecycle of an escalation – starting with the first meeting with a client that has raised the escalation, through the ongoing client meetings and negotiations phase, and finally to the resolution and closure.

Who should attend?

In general, the audience best suited to the Program are those who are in client-facing roles. They can be Engagement (e.g. Account Executives/Relationship Managers/Client Success Managers) or Project Delivery (e.g. Project Managers/Program Directors/Delivery Executives/Consultants). It suits people of all levels of experience, especially those who need to develop their skills in managing escalations.

Sessions can be tailored for the more experienced person who wants to improve their skills and expertise in handling difficult and problem situations, or for senior, experienced delivery leaders, who are strong in relationship management or program/project delivery but need to improve their handling of the commercial aspects of an escalation or dispute.

The full program has been highly successful in both a face-to-face and virtual environment.

For more information on the program, please visit www.ashleysaltzman.com.

Author: Ashley Saltzman, www.ashleysaltzman.com
Book Adviser: Jaqui Lane, www.thebookadviser.com.au
Designer: Rasika UM, www.shashika.info
© 2021 Ashley Saltzman
ISBN 978-0-6451252-1-4

This book is copyright. Apart from any fair dealing for the purposes of private study, research, criticism or review, as permitted under the Copyright Act 1968 and subsequent amendments, no part may be reproduced, stored in or introduced into a retrieval system or transmitted in any form or by any means (electronic, mechanical, photocopying, recording or otherwise) without written permission in writing from the author, Ashley Saltzman. Enquiries re bulk copy purchases should be directed to Ashley Saltzman.

www.ingramcontent.com/pod-product-compliance
Lightning Source LLC
Chambersburg PA
CBHW051453290426
44109CB00016B/1745